THE
DA VINCI
ENIGMA
TAROT

THE

DA VINCI
ENIGMA
TAROT

CAITLÍN MATTHEWS

ST. MARTIN'S PRESS
New York

This book is dedicated to John in the year he regained his full sight.
May the joy of observation enrich your understanding and experience.

AN EDDISON•SADD EDITION
Edited, designed and produced by
Eddison Sadd Editions Limited
St Chad's House, 148 King's Cross Road
London WC1X 9DH
www.eddisonsadd.com

Phototypeset in Centaur MT and Trajan using QuarkXPress on Apple Macintosh
Origination by Pixel Tech and Chroma Graphics (Overseas) Pte Ltd, Singapore
Printed and bound by CT Printing Ltd, China

CONTENTS

INTRODUCTION

EXPLORING THE ENIGMA

During the writing of this book, in January 2005, a hidden room was found during the renovations of the rambling friary of Santissima Annunziata in Florence. The room was nothing less than the lost studio of Leonardo da Vinci, complete with frescos. This incredible discovery arrived right in the middle of the *Da Vinci Code* phenomenon that has gripped the world, adding to everyone's excitement.

Since Leonardo scorned what he saw as necromancy and alchemy as 'lies', we cannot say what he would have made of all this. In a whirl of esoteric speculation, Leonardo remains, as usual, aloof, much more interested in the mysteries of the cosmos than in the Knights Templar or the Holy Grail. So why a Da Vinci tarot, and why is it an enigma?

For me, tarot is not a method of 'fortune-telling' but a way of preparing for the next moment by scrutinizing the present circumstances. Leonardo's pragmatism, his insistence upon clear and accurate observation, his distrust of speculation and his desire to extend the discoveries of the ancients by finding new pathways, have always spoken to me as the necessary requirements for a seer. His profound understanding of the soul and his sense of vocational direction and flexibility are what we all need to explore our own lives and souls – such an enigma to us still. Taken together with his immense artistry and his enquiring mind, this tarot is an attempt to provide a book of life – a portable art gallery and a tool for navigating your way through life with respect for the macrocosm of which we are a part.

There is something indefinably enigmatic about Leonardo that fuels all kinds of wild speculation, but you won't find such speculation in this tarot. I have attempted to use his own words and images and let them speak. I have even made a space for

Leonardo to ask you his own terse, acerbic questions. The images on these cards portray the range of Leonardo's vast interests. Though they may be less familiar to us than the famous paintings, they are no less iconic. Many of them have the intimacy and thoughtfulness of the unconscious artist, who draws for himself alone and not for any audience or patron. They are thus more reflective and insightful.

Working through the logistics of how Leonardo and the framework of the tarot meet, I have been aware of an accidental time resonance between Leonardo's life and my own, for he was born in 1452 and I was born in 1952. Of course, there can be no further comparison between us, save for this simple accident of age and perhaps a polymath's impatience to move on to the next thing before accomplishing the last – a kind of loss-cutting process that I'm afraid I sometimes share. But the frailties of old age are beginning for me as they did for him, and the increasing urgency to create, consolidate and leave a legacy is one with which I greatly empathize. What he would have made of it, I can't tell, but I hope his ingenious mind would have enjoyed this playful tarot, for he was not above such pursuits himself: his household accounts record *'per dire la venture: 6 soldi'*, or 'paid out 6 shillings for having the future told'.

These tarot cards follow his curious and penetrating vision through his own words and drawings to look more deeply at how the macrocosm, the Greater World of the Eternal Cosmos, and the microcosm, the created world in which we live, meet and mingle. Leonardo wrote, 'It is an easy thing to make oneself universal.' These seventy-eight cards create a portable notebook to help you explore the sacred proportions and divine harmony of the macrocosm, so that you can find balance and harmony in your everyday life.

THE DA VINCI ENIGMA TAROT

When you first pick up a tarot pack, you naturally want to know everything about it all at once. However, *The Da Vinci Enigma Tarot* will reveal itself to you over time as you play, practise, read and study it. Such a gradual unfolding is at odds with our expectations in a modern 'instant enlightenment' world, but I do urge you to persevere by making haste slowly, and savouring the art and pattern that will help reveal the enigma of your soul and its destiny. Elegant simplicity and mastery are arrived at through continual practice, just as Leonardo himself learned his craft as an apprentice in the studio of Verrocchio, his master. Leonardo wrote, 'Let those who are dismayed at the outset of their studies prepare to ... devote themselves patiently to those studies with great results.'

Section 1 invites you to visit Leonardo da Vinci, who is the master magician of this tarot, though impatient readers might be tempted to start with section 2, *Finding Your Way*, to understand the cards' unique patterns. Sections 3 and 4 explore the card meanings, which extend ordinary tarot into other realms of exploration, and section 5 gives you new card spreads to practise your readings. To help you familiarize yourself with the cards by play and practice, there are several conventional-style spreads, where you lay each card in a certain position. Then, when you know the cards a little better, you will be able to move on to the Destiny spread, which is an endlessly enticing, allusive and illuminating way of using both the face and the back of the cards. This more advanced spread will keep you enthralled and help develop and extend your powers of interpretation.

Finally, I would like to acknowledge John Matthews, who conceived the idea for this tarot. I was to have written with him, but prior commitments left him pursuing other themes, and I continued to follow its development alone. I now share this journey with you.

CAITLÍN MATTHEWS
Oxford
28 January 2005

1

LEONARDO DA VINCI

DISCIPLE OF EXPERIENCE

'You have been placed at the centre of the universe that you might more easily observe whatever is in the world. We have made you neither of heaven nor of earth, neither mortal nor immortal, so that with freedom of choice and with honour, as the maker and moulder of yourself, you may fashion yourself into whatever shape you desire ... Who would not admire this chameleon?'

— PICO DELLA MIRANDOLA, 'On the Dignity of Man'

These words of God to Adam read like the original maker's instructions to the man we know as Leonardo da Vinci. He certainly did his very best to live up to them. As a polymath of genius, he has been the inspiration of artists, scientists and mathematicians. Many have written about him, but let us first remember that he regarded himself as the *'discepolo dell'esperienza'* – 'disciple of experience' – which was the true source of his inspiration. Rather than believe what others have written about Leonardo, we can read for ourselves what he thought and believed, for his exploratory mind is known to us first-hand from his own writings. He kept notebooks throughout his life, in which to jot down ideas, impressions, sketches, observations and projects, and although these notebooks and their detached pages have been scattered to collections around the world, their evidence speaks of a unique mind and a searching soul, never ceasing to consider the experience of the universe.

Leonardo da Vinci was born on 15 April 1452, to a peasant girl named Caterina, the illegitimate first-born son of a Florentine notary, Piero da Vinci. He started life with none of the advantages a well-born son might have expected. Poorly educated, he was trained not for his father's office, but rather apprenticed to the studio-school of the artist Andrea del Verrocchio, where his exceptional eye and draftsmanship were quickly recognized by the likes of Lorenzo de' Medici.

It was probably Lorenzo de' Medici who assisted Leonardo in moving on from his youthful troubles in Florence – a narrowly averted prosecution for homosexuality in 1476 and an unfinished commission for *The Adoration of the Magi* – and to seek the service of Ludovico Sforza, Duke of Milan. Leonardo wrote a letter of astonishing chutzpah to the warlike Sforza, outlining his own technical prowess in the building of new military engines, and only latterly detailing his artistic ability. It was during his seventeen years in Milan that Leonardo's career was formed, for Sforza gave him freedom to develop his ideas.

Leonardo was friends with many of the glitterati of his day, including the Medici's pet painter, Botticelli (whose paintings Leonardo hated), and the Renaissance spin doctor and political theorist, Niccolò Machiavelli. He had almost no close relationships with other painters, notably disagreeing violently with Michelangelo. Leonardo's immense self-conceit unseated any other artist from the pinnacle of greatness. But then Michelangelo was only a half-fledged humanist, with the piety of a medieval Christian, whereas Leonardo's humanism was hard-headed and coolly pragmatic. Leonardo's friendship with Machiavelli was based upon a mutual and empirical observation of how things worked. It was only the work of the young Raphael that moved him, towards the end of his life.

After an unsettled career in which he constantly sought patrons to support him, Leonardo entered the service of Pope Leo X in 1513. But here in Rome, his anatomical studies were denounced as 'necromancy' by the assistants lent to him by the Pope. Leo X banned him from further experiment.

Leonardo was lucky to have enjoyed his career in a relatively liberal period, but ecclesiastical views of humanism and scientific experiment were to become much narrower as the century proceeded. Shortly afterwards Leonardo was presented to the young and vigorous French king, Francis I, who was so delighted with Leonardo that he invited him to live in France. Leonardo moved there in 1516, dying at Amboise in 1519 at the age of 67.

A RENAISSANCE MAN

Leonardo was a Renaissance man in all senses of the term: a polymath blessed with multi-talented gifts that he explored and manifested, creating a synthesis of disciplines that is truly inspirational. Few artists have enjoyed a career so varied and influential, for he was not only a painter, sculptor and musician, but an engineer, overseer of water-works and canals, inventor, natural historian, original thinker and philosopher, as well as a theoretical scientist. In a world which looks to science to explain mysteries and improve the human condition, the fascination for Leonardo's prophetic vision of 'things to come' remains constant. His interest in the natural world led his discerning eye to observe and delineate the forms and qualities of life, not just in a rational manner, on the surface, but also to reveal the harmony, beauty and order of its innate pattern.

The world of the Renaissance serves as a backdrop to Leonardo's brilliance; a time when new ideas such as humanism, scientific understanding of the cosmos and personal destiny began to question the received wisdom of the Church, which ruled by dogma rather than experience. He created the blueprints for many ideas and arte-facts we now take for granted, including manned flight, the submersible, the diving bell, helicopters, tanks, steam power, advanced hydraulics, plastic and contact lenses, as well as the camera obscura, which preceded the modern camera. These remarkable inventions outstripped the conventions of these innovative times, where peering too intently into the mainspring of the universe was tantamount to heresy. Leonardo's soaring mind overflies these forbidden territories, striving to find the truth by which life may be lived. The moral dilemmas between belief and the usages of science are still familiar debating points today.

The received scientific understanding of Leonardo's day was based upon the writings of such influential scholars as Aristotle. But Leonardo clearly saw how many Classical scientific theories were erroneous due to faulty observation. As a self-styled disciple of experience, he was led by his artistic eye and his own painstaking observa-tion to other conclusions: 'my proofs contradict the authority of certain respected men who are looked up to because of their inexperienced judgements'. He held that 'all of our knowledge has its origin in our perceptions'.

Leonardo was a man of extreme contradictions: a hater of war who designed weapons of destruction; a vegetarian who dissected animals and humans for anatomical research; a great painter who rarely finished commissions; an incipient humanist who believed in God; a man who questioned the received knowledge of Classical writers but who nevertheless read them avidly; one who served powerful masters but whose own mastery surpassed theirs; one who saw the divine in the human but who was often scornful of humanity.

Despite the idolatry bestowed upon his memory, Leonardo was as human as his fellow men, even accused in his youth of homosexual liaisons at a time when the mandatory sentence for sodomy was death. That he escaped public trial and execution is fortunate for all who esteem his work. If any of his notebooks had become known, Leonardo's far-seeing scientific theories and his heretical scorn of some of the Church's practices would have surely led to excommunication and death. Leonardo's secrecy was his security, and may partially account for the way in which he made his notes, in mirror writing.

This cryptic habit was not unique to him, since it was also used a generation or so earlier by the artist Filippo Brunelleschi, who solved the architectural puzzle of how to create a dome to cap the unfinished cathedral in Florence; in order to hide his controversial plans from the many rivals contending for the same commission, Brunelleschi kept them strictly secret by recording his notes in mirror writing. It is evident from handwriting samples that the left-handed Leonardo found it easier to write backwards rather than forwards. A left-handed genius in a world of right-handed men, an unacknowledged and marginalized illegitimate son in a world of true-born citizens, Leonardo carved his own destiny in a way that lesser conventional men could not.

FROM HUMBLE BEGINNINGS ...

We tend to look up to Leonardo as an intellectual giant, but that was not how he began. As an illegitimate son, his education was so negligible that he had no Latin or mathematics. When he came to Florence to mix in the urbane and educated circles of the sophisticated banking family of the Medici, he was at a distinct disadvantage.

Other intellectual luminaries preceded him, and perhaps looked down upon this good-looking but unproved youth with the countrified accent. Men like Marsilio Ficino, the Neo-Platonist who translated the works of Plato and the *Corpus Hermeticum* for the great Cosimo de' Medici, or the poet Angelo Poliziano, Leonardo's contemporary, or even the astoundingly learned Pico della Mirandola, who studied the esoteric arts of Kabbala as well as exploring the new humanism which appealed to Leonardo: such men as this headed Cosimo's Academy, founded after the example of Plato, where minds could meet in symposia to discuss vital philosophic and learned matters.

Over the door of Plato's original Academy was the warning, 'Let no one enter here who is ignorant of geometry.' This pretty much excluded Leonardo, who subsequently made mathematics and geometry his life's task to master, at one point becoming so absorbed in their study that he had no time or interest in prestigious commissions. He found the teachings of the great mathematician Luca Pacioli supremely inspiring. While Leonardo was in the service of Sforza, he illustrated Pacioli's book *The Divine Proportion*, with three-dimensional drawings of Platonic solids.

Unable to compete with the learned Pico or Poliziano, Leonardo originated a wholly new and original study: the observation of nature and experience. He wanted to establish a unique mixture of art and science, in which all artists would observe the structure and form of everything, recording it *how it was*. In this, he alone was uniquely qualified, but it did not stop him dreaming. There is a design which he may have intended as a suitable and punning logo on his own name, 'Da Vinci', which also means 'of the osiers', showing a circular interwoven design enclosing an ambitious but certainly never fulfilled plan. It reads 'Academia Leonardi Vinci' ('Leonardo da Vinci's Academy'). This emblem seems evidence of a pipe-dream, for it is doubtful whether Leonardo had the patience, application or sustained interest to teach students.

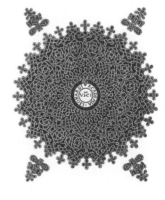

Like many of his ideas, Leonardo's Academy was conceived by a brilliant mind that could not always fulfil its ambitious promise, whether due to an unrealized theoretical approach or to the technical constraints of the time. Ironically, it fell to the painter Raphael to portray Leonardo as the head of the Academy. In Raphael's 1509 fresco *The School of Athens*, the elderly Leonardo is portrayed centre stage as Plato himself, with a copy of the *Timaeus* under his arm and a characteristic upward-pointing right index finger, while Michelangelo huddles moodily on the steps in the foreground as the philosopher Heraclitus.

THE ENIGMA OF THE SOUL

Throughout a number of Leonardo's paintings an enigmatic feature continually recurs: the pointing finger. It appears in some of the cards in this tarot deck, including VI Twins, XI Experience and XVII Way-Shower. It is also appears in his paintings *The Last Supper*, *St John the Baptist* and *The Virgin of the Rocks* (in the Louvre version). What does this pointing finger signify? In the VI Twins card, it looks as if St Anne is reminding her daughter Mary that Jesus is not merely her child but is born for a higher purpose. In the XVII Way-Shower card, it is evident that St John the Baptist (who also appears in VI Twins) is doing his prophetic best to announce the way of the Lord. But what of the mysterious pointing woman in the XI Experience card? She points to the mystery that is the soul's enigma, which we comprehend only by means of our unique experience of life.

Everyone's soul is an enigma waiting to be read. Destiny is not a fixed or fated pathway, but an unfolding blueprint that we each discover as we experience life. There is a treasury of gifts within each of us that helps us read the enigma of our unique code. The way we use these gifts and weave them together helps determine our ultimate pathway through life. By knowing ourselves, by looking more intently at the reasons why we were born, we discover our unique soul's signature, becoming more harmoniously aligned with the universe. In an era where the importance of physical DNA is universally acknowledged, it is extraordinary that the soul's unique code is so neglected. Leonardo's vision of an integrated macrocosm and microcosm seems to point to his struggle to understand the interrelationship of body and soul.

Within Leonardo is an angelic twin, the soul who explores further than than the physical frame can extend. This internal duality between the man and his genius is portrayed many times in his art, in such paintings as the *Madonna of the Rocks*, where Christ and St John the Baptist are shown together as children. Part of Leonardo is like St John the Baptist – a way-shower who looks ahead and prepares the way for a greater one than himself. But the other part of Leonardo is like Christ, striving with his humanity to realize his divinity, aiming to achieve the highest principles of clarity and illumination (*see VI Twins*).

In his *On the Dignity of Man*, Pico della Mirandola wrote, quoting the Chaldean prophet Zoroaster, 'the soul has wings but when the feathers fall off, she is conveyed immediately into the body. When the wings sprout again, she flies up the heavens.' When Zoroaster was asked by his students how to obtain soul-wings that will fly well, he advised them to 'moisten the wings with the waters of life'.

In Leonardo we distinguish a soul whose wings fell off. He sought for them all his life, yearning to fly again. And if anyone ever deserved to fly, it was this complex, brilliant, impatient man who moistened his dream-wings in the waters of life so well that his flight is still not over. He has lent wings to all who aspire, explore and observe.

2

FINDING YOUR WAY

THE DA VINCI ENIGMA TAROT

'From my own experience, I have discovered that it is of no small benefit to review the forms that you have been studying in your imagination as you lie in bed in the dark, considering the significant things that arise from such subtle perception. This is a most valuable exercise, very useful in imprinting things upon the memory.'

— LEONARDO DA VINCI

This chapter offers a quick overview of the layout and shape of *The Da Vinci Enigma Tarot*. If you are already familiar with tarot, you will immediately be able to see here how it differs from, and corresponds to, a conventional pack. (NOTE: If this is your first tarot, you may find a general beginner's tarot book helpful for information on the history and overall perspective of tarot. See Further Reading, page 144.)

The Da Vinci Enigma Tarot is nothing less than a map of the cosmos, comprising macrocosm and microcosm. This is a Renaissance way of seeing the cosmos, with the macrocosm, or 'Greater World', as the entire universe seen as a whole, and the microcosm, or 'Lesser World', as the reflection of the macrocosm in miniature. In the Renaissance philosophy of Leonardo, the microcosm was the human being: 'the ancients called man a lesser world … [for he] … is composed of earth, water, air and fire'. By attempting to harmonize microcosm with macrocosm, we are enabled to live in a more coherent way that is faithful to the union of both worlds. This union is shown in XXI World.

In addition to the tarot deck of seventy-eight cards, you will find two Enigma Cards, unique to this deck. The first of these reveals how the card-backs (including these two cards) join together to make a complete pattern. This pattern, with its repeating roundels and interlacing knotwork, is similar to the labyrinthine repeat design that Leonardo used to decorate the Sala della Asse in Ludovico Sforza's castle in Milan, and is also the central design featured in his own 'Academia' emblem (*see page* 13). Across the Enigma Pattern design are five repeating poly-hedra, or many-sided geometric forms, which Leonardo drew for Luca Pacioli, his mathematical mentor, in his 1509 book *The Divine Proportion*.

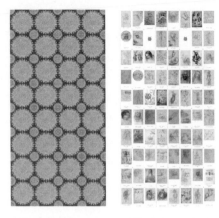

The Enigma Pattern   The Enigma Grid

In his *Timaeus*, which speaks of the formation of the cosmos, Plato deduced that it is composed of four elements – Air, Fire, Water and Earth – and that these are associated with four polyhedra, or Platonic solids. 'We assign the cube (Hexahedron) to earth, for it is the most immobile and the most retentive of shape. The least mobile (Icosahedron) we assign to water, the most mobile (Tetrahedron) to fire and the intermediate (Octahedron) to air. There remains a fifth construction which the god used to embroider the constellations on the whole heaven (the Dodecahedron).' The significance of these four elemental forms and the Dodecahedron, which repre-sents spirit, will become clear later on, when you come to use the Destiny spread (*see page* 137).

The second Enigma Card features the Enigma Grid, which shows the sequence of the full deck face up. This grid replicates the interpenetration of the microcosm with the macrocosm, and reveals the natural 'resting places' for the cards, if they were to come together as a complete deck. When you use the Destiny spread, you will learn how matching the card-backs together produces a series of random connections that *transcend* the Enigma Grid sequence, helping you find the unique signature of your soul's code. The two Enigma Cards are not used in play, but only for reference. All sacred patterns have this empty space within them to allow divine inspiration to inspirit whatever is created.

THE MACROCOSM CARDS

The twenty-two Major Arcana cards form the greater archetypal world of the macrocosm, containing the primal patterns of all existence. These cards are drawn from Leonardo's sketches and studies for his paintings. They portray the major influences that affect every living person, initiations that are essential for a balanced life. When you receive macrocosm cards in a reading, look carefully at the major influences they reveal in your destiny. Twelve cards receive new names in this tarot.

DA VINCI ENIGMA NAME	CONVENTIONAL NAME	DA VINCI ENIGMA NAME	CONVENTIONAL NAME
0 Fool	0 Fool	XI Experience	XI Justice
I Magician	I Magician	XII Passover	XII Hanged Man
II Enigma	II High Priestess	XIII Death	XIII Death
III Empress	III Empress	XIV Temperance	XIV Temperance
IV Emperor	IV Emperor	XV Pain & Pleasure	XV Devil
V Hierophant	V Hierophant	XVI Deluge	XVI Tower
VI Twins	VI Lovers	XVII Way-Shower	XVII Star
VII Imagination	VII Chariot	XVIII Conception	XVIII Moon
VIII Strength	VIII Strength	XIX Birth	XIX Sun
IX Hermit	IX Hermit	XX Renewal	XX Last Judgement
X Time	X Wheel of Fortune	XIX World	XXI World

THE MICROCOSM CARDS

The fifty-six Minor Arcana cards form the lesser world of the microcosm, comprising the manifest forms of existence and the pathways that each of our unique gifts can take. The manifest world of the microcosm mirrors and reflects the greater world of the macrocosm. The four elements of Air, Fire, Water and Earth form the four traditional suits of Swords, Wands, Cups and Coins (or Pentacles) respectively, though other fourfold qualities important to Leonardo are also present. He speaks of our bones as rocks, and the circulation of blood and breath as the tides of the ocean. Leonardo saw the four powers of nature as Percussion, Force, Impetus and Weight: they are 'the children of movement since they are born of it' (*see right*).

TRADITIONAL SUIT	DA VINCI ENIGMA SUIT	POWER OF NATURE
Swords	Air	Percussion
Wands	Fire	Force
Cups	Water	Impetus
Coins	Earth	Weight

AIR The Air suit is courageous, even brash, not afraid to show its strength. It cuts forthrightly through to the heart of the matter and shows the mind and actions of the warrior and leader. It is associated with the principle of *percussion*, which humans experience as blows.

FIRE The Fire suit is full of invention and energy, exploring the creative source that shapes the soul's destiny. The suit demonstrates the applications of the artisan to his craft. These cards show the principle of *force*, which human beings experience as power.

WATER This suit concerns the feelings and flow of our soul's destiny. It reveals our love and engagement with our life's path, as well as the artist's sense of aesthetic. This suit is associated with the principle of *impetus*, which humans experience as flow or motion.

EARTH This suit represents the work of our hands, and shows how you engage with the vocational gift of the soul's path. The cards reveal how our soul's gift is manifested in daily life through business and transaction. This suit is associated with the principle of *weight*, which human beings experience as gravity.

The cards numbered Ace to Ten are drawn from Leonardo's notebooks, wherein he sketched his inventions, dissections, theories and observations about the natural world. The number cards in your readings usually represent the flow of life, your intentions, attitudes and actions. Each number card has a name:

	AIR	FIRE	WATER	EARTH
ACE	Air	Fire	Water	Earth
TWO	Respect	Direction	Union	Polarity
THREE	Trials	Matrix	Conjunction	Perspective
FOUR	Repose	Celebration	Disappointment	Assembly
FIVE	Contention	Struggle	Unwinding	Need
SIX	Flowering	Victory	Memory	Giving
SEVEN	Action	Success	Illusion	Stamina
EIGHT	Confinement	Trajectory	Transport	Labour
NINE	Danger	Repelling	Airborne	Roots
TEN	Punishment	Burdens	Family	Foundation

- *Aces* concern beginnings, causes, primal energies and empowerments.
- *Twos* show duality, thresholds, promises and accords.
- *Threes* reveal the fruits of Twos: plans, affirmations, understandings.
- *Fours* show opportunities, early manifestions, first stabilities and meetings.
- *Fives* concern clarifications, modifications, challenges and break-downs.
- *Sixes* reveal attunements, achievements and harmonious correspondences.
- *Sevens* show the imaginations, and the effect of actions and attitudes.
- *Eights* concern reappraisals or intentions and movements that arise from Sevens.
- *Nines* reveal integration, flexibility and accomplishments.
- *Tens* show culmination, conclusion and final manifestion.

The Court Cards The court cards of each of the elemental suits derive from Leonardo's many drawings for portraits, masques and fantasies. When you find court cards in your readings, they represent people or attitudes that are at work in your issue. The court cards in this tarot are Page, Knight, Lady and Lord. There are no kings or queens because the Italian city-states of Leonardo's time were republics rather than kingdoms.

UNDERSTANDING THE CARD MEANINGS

Each of the card interpretations in this book describes the card image and includes the following sections:

DIMMI Throughout the margins of his notebooks, Leonardo uses the phrase *'dimmi'*, or 'tell me', whenever he tries out a new pen-nib, as if challenging it to tell him something new. Each card asks you one or two questions about the card you've drawn, which *you* answer in relation to the issue you are reading for. Engage with these questions as honestly as you can: they will tell you much more than the given meanings in this book.

BACKGROUND This gives information about the card and some biographical information about Leonardo's life and works or the subject of the card.

SOUL-CODE This reveals how the chosen card helps or challenges your soul's destiny. When you are learning about the cards, use this paragraph for meditation. If you are trying hard to interpret a card, you will find both this and the dimmi questions helpful in unlocking what the card is about. When you lay the Destiny spread, you can use the soul-code information to help 'bridge' your connected and disconnected cards.

UPRIGHT In conventional spreads, read this if your card is upright. In the Destiny spread, read this meaning if your card is upright and connects to another one.

REVERSED In conventional spreads, read this for any reversed cards. In the Destiny spread, read this for any cards that you've had to reverse to make a connected set. If your card is both disconnected *and* reversed, look at both meanings.

DISCONNECTED In conventional spreads, you might not use this meaning at all. However, if you find a card 'difficult' or you have an inner ambivalence about it, then try consulting this. In the Destiny spread, you read this meaning for any cards that cannot be incorporated into the connected set(s).

QUESTIONS AND DIVINATION ISSUES

The issues that lead us to divine are as various and individual as we are. 'Divination' means 'to ask the gods', and the questions that we put to the tarot are ones to which we need urgent and essential answers. These answers arrive from two places: from the macrocosmic perspective that is wider than the merely human viewpoint, and also from the microcosm of our own deepest intuition. We often already know the answers or the means to a solution, but it isn't until we have tested this intuition that we believe it. Here, divination becomes validation. Our destiny is not fatally sealed or predetermined, but rather navigable by means of the question. If we keep checking coordinates we will steer towards our star, keeping our 'unwavering course'. (*See also Two of Fire, page 86.*)

The way in which we ask questions of the tarot is the whole key to tarot-reading. Without a useful, searching question we will not get a decent answer that can help us. Ponder your issue carefully to prepare your question, and write it down. Look at what you've written – does it state what you really mean? The following tips will help you make sure you're asking the right questions.

1 Keep your question concise and to the point. Choose an issue that is urgent rather than one asked out of curiosity.
2 Avoid questions giving yes/no answers. For instance, instead of asking 'Shall we go and live in another country?', reframe this question as 'What are the consequences of going to live in another country?'
3 Frame your question in a positive rather than negative way. So, rather than asking 'Why am I failing?', ask 'How can I succeed?'

Here are some useful question frames for your issues:
• Please give me clarity about [the issue].
• Please show me the next step in this process.
• Please help me understand [the issue].
• What's the most important thing to focus on here?

HOW TO USE THE CARDS

Handling the Cards Some people find shuffling very difficult and prefer to draw cards unseen out of the pack, or to mix the cards around on a table or on the floor. Whichever method you choose, when you are ready to lay your cards down face up, do ensure that you turn them over sideways rather than flipping them 'foot over head', or you could end up inadvertently placing an upright card down in the reversed position. Additionally, when you turn over cards in the Destiny spread you will also need to turn them mirrorwise (*see page* 138).

Finding Guide Cards After you've composed your question for the cards, shuffle your issue into the whole pack. When you've finished shuffling, lay the cards face down and cut them into three relatively even piles, from right to left. Turn the piles over and note the card at the bottom of each pile. These three Guide Cards can be very helpful in setting the tone of the reading, and may appear as guiding principles that signpost the issues involved. Note these, putting them back where you found them. Then turn the three piles back down and reassemble the pack into one again (picking up the piles from left to right, to retain the cut), drawing the cards off the top to make your reading. The sample spreads in section 5 reveal how these Guide Cards work.

Reversed Cards Some tarot users are confused by or impatient with reversed cards, and choose always to use upright meanings; I know that I did when I first used tarot. However, to fully explore the enigma of your soul's code, you will find that you get more out of your readings if you use reversed cards. Not all reversed cards are difficult or unpleasant: some bring alleviation of distress, such as Four of Water. If you are a careful shuffler you will not always accidentally generate any reversals. To create some random reversals, therefore, hold the whole deck (with cards upright) in one hand, and with one finger of the other hand push up as many cards as your fingertip displaces. Remove these cards, reverse them and randomly shuffle or place them one at a time back into the pack. When you use the Destiny spread, you will automatically create reversals when you try to connect cards into part of the Enigma Pattern.

Clearing the Cards When you have finished a reading, it is a good idea to 'clear the cards', so that the card-sequence and influence of the last question or querent (the person asking the question) are thoroughly dispersed. You will find that the cards you've just used tend to be a bit 'sticky', and will show up in reading after reading otherwise. If you are going to lay another spread immediately following the first, then put the cards you've used back into the deck at random intervals. When you've finished reading, deal out the deck of upright cards onto seven piles, as if dealing seven hands of cards, and pick these up in random order, which will both clear and remix them. To read again, make a new selection of reversed cards.

Augmenting and Bridging Many tarot readers take the next card from the pack when they need to amplify a card that's difficult to interpret or understand. This is said to 'augment' a card. You can lay the new card directly upon or beside a 'difficult' card. When you do this, read the soul-code meanings for both cards to help give you guidance. In the Destiny spread, you are encouraged to draw a random card to help bridge any disconnected cards and bring them back into your reading.

Interpreting the Cards The interpretation of cards is an art that cannot be taught in a book, since there are always three factors in any tarot-reading: the querent, the question and the cards themselves. It is only by applying these three facets together, and leaving yourself – the reader – out of things, that you can arrive at an interpretation. Always relate the cards to the question that you or the querent asked. This will help you to keep focused on the answers given. When reading for other people, try using the dimmi questions to generate a response from them rather than merely reading the given meanings. This sparks amazing results, I assure you.

The meanings of the cards in *The Da Vinci Enigma Tarot* have been personalized for the lone reader who wants to decode the enigma of the soul. If you are reading for someone else, then the focus is upon that person or situation, and you will have to moderate the meanings to reflect this. The card meanings are not set in stone but will reveal many new aspects as you read for different issues and individuals.

3

MACROCOSM CARDS

THE GREATER ARCHETYPAL WORLD

'It is an easy thing to make oneself universal.'

— LEONARDO DA VINCI

0 FOOL

0 FOOL

DIMMI

What is calling you to follow this new departure?
How does instinct empower you?

A RAGGED BEGGAR IN FETTERS

BACKGROUND The greater part of Leonardo's artistic life was one of struggle, of managing to live hand to mouth, forever at the beck and call of patrons and municipal authorities who held the purse-strings. We occasionally catch a glimpse of his barely reined-in impatience with the demands of wrangling civil servants, querulous church dignitaries and the imperiousness of princely commands. When he first set out to make his fortune in the court of Ludovico Sforza in Milan, he was presented, extraordinarily, not as an artist but as a musician. Aware of his own potential and desirous of catching the eye of a powerful patron, Leonardo put himself forward as military engineer who could create weapons and defences that would overthrow and repel enemies in a very overweening proposal. He offers to lay his skills and 'his secrets' at the disposal of Sforza, to create engines and unknown machines such as armoured cars and cannons that will hail destruction upon the enemy. This risky, over-confident account of his untried abilities was somehow accepted, and he was launched in Milan as a valued member of Sforza's following.

This element of risk, and of biting off more than was possible to achieve, marked Leonardo's whole career. This beggar is one of his designs for one of the extravagant masques of Sforza, for whom the budding artist undertook many menial tasks, such as the central heating of the duchess's bathroom, among others. The beggar in this card is fettered by ignorance and constrained by the will of another, but he has an imagination that flies free of his fetters. He seeks knowledge and freedom, longing for a wider, more generous world to live in where he can stretch his abilities to the full.

SOUL-CODE Instinct is the first guide to life. Listen to what your gut instinct is telling you about this situation. Public opinion is not necessarily a good indication of how you should proceed in this matter. If you feel the stir of a journey without a fixed destination, set your foot upon the path and initiate your destiny. The way will not always be as clear and easy as it now appears, but return to what triggered you to go forth and you will soon pick up the track.

UPRIGHT A naive and childlike delight leads you into new projects and themes with a rush of enthusiasm. Innocence and spontaneity can carry you much of the way. There is a yearning for freedom and new vistas, and you follow your vision despite lack of resources.

REVERSED It seems grown-up to avoid risks, but you must venture yourself sometime and risk being seen to be a fool. Alternatively, you may already be living down a bad decision or indiscretion. An acceptance of limits keeps you hobbled. You are on a fool's errand.

DISCONNECTED You have a sense of unfettered freedom, but it is not as free as it may seem. Opportunities are not coming your way because you are still tied to a conventional outlook. Seeking the safety of limitation, you may miss the moment.

I MAGICIAN

I MAGICIAN

DIMMI

How does your unique gift change the world about you? How are you practising and maintaining your skills in everyday life?

A SELF-PORTRAIT OF LEONARDO

BACKGROUND This self-portrait in red chalk is one of the most famous images of Leonardo, shown here in his mid-sixties, possibly during his years of retirement in France. This unsparing depiction of age is in no way pathetic nor decrepit. Da Vinci's shrewd, far-seeing eyes look keenly at what he has wrought and the line of his mouth shows fiery determination, while his abundant long hair and beard are reminders of what a beautiful man he had once been. Considering the role and reputation of a painter, Leonardo writes, 'Surely it is no great achievement to attain to some perfection, especially after studying only one thing throughout his lifetime.' This is not an accusation he could level against himself – he who explored so many different avenues of art and learning. Rather, he counsels other artists, 'ensure that nothing remains in your work that is not informed by reason and by the effects found in nature ... this then is the way to make yourself renowned in your art.'

Leonardo's mature face, with the lines of experience and wisdom upon it, looks at the destiny he has skilfully accomplished. He mused, 'Whatever it is, the soul is a divine thing, so let it abide in its workings and be comfortable there ... It takes leave of the body most unwillingly.' As the magician who has created so many wonderful inventions and devices, he imparts the skill of artistry.

SOUL-CODE Originality is the key to respecting your soul's destiny. The reason that you were born is to use the skills with which you are gifted. Staying true to your originality gives you an authenticity that doesn't have to be faked or acquired because it is innately part of you. This royal road to mastery lies beneath your feet, if you will but make the journey.

UPRIGHT Skill, mastery, self-confidence are yours. You have the ability to bring things into manifestation through your skills and abilities. If you yoke clear intention and willpower to dexterity and concentration, you can achieve your plan. By adaptation, flexibility and wit, your charismatic charms can make magic. Communication and conscious intention are important now.

REVERSED Your skills and resources are not adequate for the job, nor will they deceive others for long. Over-confidence and a desire to manipulate events leads you to act like a charming trickster who beguiles the innocent while achieving your own ends. Sometimes you begin things and don't have the focus to follow them through.

DISCONNECTED Some part of you is unconscious, making you susceptible to deception. By not communicating your needs you can mislead or become overlooked. Your disconnection from your skills and abilities leaves you with a sense of inadequacy and lack of confidence. Reconnect with your powers and avoid self-sabotage.

II ENIGMA

II ENIGMA

DIMMI

What wisdom do you read in the book of your soul?
How must you apply it in this matter?

AN EARLY STUDY OF THE MONA LISA

BACKGROUND More ink has been spilt over theories concerning the identity and painting of the *Mona Lisa* than any of Leonardo's other works. We know that it was a portrait he worked at and kept with him for many years. The enigmatic smile of the *Mona Lisa*, who is also known as *La Gioconda*, or 'The Playful One', hints at the mystery of the soul but keeps her secret well. This particularly unusual study of the *Mona Lisa* shows her with the ghost of a palm frond in her hand, as if Leonardo were toying with the idea of portraying her as a martyred saint. But the palm can also represent virtue, and was used to represent a virgin, as it does on the back of Leonardo's wedding portrait of the young Ginevra da Benci, painted for her husband. The title 'Mona' is merely short for 'madonna', or 'my lady'. Lady Lisa was most likely Lisa di Antonio Maria Gherardini, daughter of a wealthy Florentine, who married Francesco di Bartolomeo del Giocondo in 1495.

But why was the finished picture still in Leonardo's hands when he was in France in 1517? We know that he overworked it continuously and did not make copies of the final painting, as he did with many others. *La Gioconda* retains her secrets still. She represents the inspirer who awakens destiny and who imparts the inspiration of spiritual wisdom, for 'wisdom is the highest good'.

SOUL-CODE The mystery of the soul's destiny is an enigma waiting to be understood. It cannot be unravelled or decoded in a mechanical way, but only by recognizing the clues and hints that intuition provides. Your soul is a unique mystery that is explored in dream or quiet reflection, in the sacred moments where your soul and the divine source are at one. Midwife your mystery in secret and do not cast it before the unappreciative and ignorant.

UPRIGHT Wisdom and prudence enable you to make intuitive links through which help may come. Self-knowledge brings serenity and discretion. Use your deep perception to penetrate to the heart of things, but respect the essential nature of what you scrutinize. You receive council or guidance.

REVERSED Shallowness and superficiality banish wisdom. Accepting the surface impression may not let you see the whole picture. Be careful not to use your insight and knowledge in destructive ways, exposing others. Your innate integrity is at risk, or you desert your core wisdom.

DISCONNECTED Unveiling the mystery of your soul before others only leads to misunderstanding and accusations of elitism or esotericism. But the 'otherness' that people see in you does not have to divide you. For you, reconnection comes from exploring that deep soul place in more detail, and from a less selfish perspective.

III EMPRESS

III EMPRESS

DIMMI

How do you take up your unique place as a living being? Where can you guide others with love and kindness in this matter?

STUDY OF ST ANNE

BACKGROUND Leonardo's study for St Anne shows the mother of Mary looking indulgently upon her grandchild, Jesus. Leonardo's major paintings and commissions involving the Holy Family remarkably show only the mother and grandmother of Christ and never St Joseph, his nominal father. Leonardo's own mother, Caterina, was a peasant girl, not married to his father. She was married off to someone of her own class, leaving Leonardo to find his way through the world as an illegitimate son who would never inherit his father's legacy. His father married successive wives, who were left with the raising of Leonardo, and this early female tenderness remains a striking feature of all his depictions of the Virgin.

The capable mother who provides everything and loves her child unstintingly was a figure not only of everyday life. In his 'prophecies', Leonardo sagely notes an ancient Mediterranean predisposition in Italy for the divine feminine over the divine masculine when it came to actual worship: 'There are many who uphold the faith of the son but only build temples in the name of the mother.' St Anne is traditionally regarded as the supreme imparter of practical wisdom, revealing that her roots stretch back to all the great goddesses of Classical culture that preceded Christianity: Rhea, Cybele, and the Great Mother herself. The tenderness of St Anne portrays the mother's love that nurtures the soul's gift.

SOUL-CODE By being faithful to the laws of life, your soul can enter into the joys and pleasures of existence, finding rhythm and timeliness. The path of a creator is nourished by generosity and patience, by allowing things to assume their innate nature in their own way. Life is your soul's opportunity to manifest your destiny by means of practical wisdom. The deep faithfulness with which you mate or mother what you encounter along your way acclaims you as one concerned with the evolution of life.

UPRIGHT Fertility and nurture bring forth the accomplishment of your plans. By giving time for things to find their natural level of growth, you foster their development and reap the harvest. The creative life-force pours into the situation, bringing satisfaction. You have the gift to create beauty and to reassure the anxious.

REVERSED Resources are not being used wisely, leading to loss, excess or wastefulness. Expediency and lack of practical planning prevent the accomplishment of your desires. Self-love or self-indulgent sensuality disempowers you and blights your relationship for others. Do not destroy what you love.

DISCONNECTED Frustrated creativity may leave you feeling full of ideas and paralysed by lack of accomplishment, or perhaps you are at an impasse where your mental and active efforts make no difference. Access your feminine side, accepting that some things must be given room to grow. Seek the medicinal nurture of beauty without feeling self-indulgent.

IV EMPEROR

IV EMPEROR

DIMMI

Where is the authority in your life? What are the boundaries of safety and order in this matter?

STUDY OF A MAN WITH HELMET

BACKGROUND This drawing dates from the early days when Leonardo was still an assistant in the workshop of Andrea del Verrocchio, where he learned his craft. It shows a mixture of skill and invention for, though the sitter is evidently a real (but unknown) man, the fantastic armour is the product of Leonardo's imagination. It is possible that it represents the Venetian *condottiere*, Colleoni, or some other commander of troops. This stern, patriarchal warrior could represent one of the many powerful leaders of the Italian city-states who patronized Leonardo, hard men accustomed to command – men like Ludovico Sforza or Cesare Borgia.

Although we think of the Renaissance as a time of cultural innovation, it was also a troubled era of military opportunism and civic expansion, needing strong leaders who could be shrewd and firm. The leaders of the city-states had to keep an unwavering dictatorial hand upon their citizens, plying them with rewards and meting out punishments in a godfatherly manner. Leonardo's letter of recommendation of Ludovico Sforza, Duke of Milan, stresses Da Vinci's availability as the foremost 'inventor of instruments of war', and only afterwards as one who 'in peaceful times can give perfect satisfaction' as an architect, sculptor and painter. In a time of turmoil, only the strong survived – men who were virtual dictators, about to wield power and command loyalty. The Emperor portrays the father's discipline necessary to guide the soul's gift.

SOUL-CODE The soul does not apologize for its destiny but follows its course from start to finish with conviction and authority. This powerful pathway is attained not by ignoring others upon the way, but by a skilful and far-sighted use of safe boundaries and good order, and by taking responsibility for decisions and plans. It is not by force that the destined goal is reached, but by self-mastery and responsibility. The way in which you father or protect acclaims you as one who brings a virile and energetic responsibility which guards all things living.

UPRIGHT Authority comes from power, which you possess in abundance. Capability and competence bring stability. Leadership comes naturally when it is based upon assurance and conviction; these qualities make things safe for those in your care. Strong parameters maintain good order. Set your sights and allocate resources accordingly.

REVERSED Impotence and immaturity betray your principles. Autocracy, prejudice or immaturity sap your power, rendering you dominating and ineffective. Emotionally closed down, you can still find the benevolence and compassion to seek firm but lasting solutions without oppressing others.

DISCONNECTED Too much dependence upon reason, logic and the dogmatic assertion of your views can isolate you. Or perhaps you feel oppressed or abused by a source of authority that holds you in thrall? Self-worth must be stimulated so that you can inhabit your own authority and mastery.

V HIEROPHANT

V HIEROPHANT

DIMMI

How do you bridge the microcosm of daily life with the macrocosm of spiritual existence? How can you mediate between the imponderable or irreconcilable things in this matter?

STUDY OF ST PETER FOR THE LAST SUPPER FRESCO

BACKGROUND The career of the first pope, St Peter, passes from that of simple fisherman to supreme pontiff of the Christian world. As Christ's first follower, Peter is the stone (*petrus*) upon which he built his church. As hierophant, he is literally a bridge (or pontiff) leading to salvation, but he began as a humble fisherman, who only later became 'a fisher of men'. However, in Leonardo's time, the papal court was categorized by great intrigue and dereliction of spiritual duty. The war-like Pope Julius II realized that the only way to provide for his military campaigns and ambitious building projects was through the sale of indulgences, a practice followed by Leo X. Licensed priests went out through the land selling indulgences to the faithful, who might thus buy themselves or others out of time spent in purgatory. The sale of indulgences was one of the practices that subsequently fuelled the Reformation. Leonardo wrote about this abuse, complaining that this was done 'without permission of the Master of these things, by those who had not the power nor authority to sell them'. Leonardo worked for Pope Leo X, but did not relish his time in Rome, where his anatomical studies brought charges of 'necromancy'.

The traditional triple crown of the hierophant represents the fusion of priestly, prophetic and kingly roles, or pope as universal pastor, ecclesiastical judge and temporal ruler. Leonardo depicts Christ's first disciple as the revealer of the soul's destiny through the path of practical experience.

SOUL-CODE The soul seeks for channels of spiritual truth and sources of sacred illumination to help find a way through life. It is not through religion alone, but through
deeply moral ideologies, lifestyles and beliefs that the soul finds the necessary synthesis to honour both macrocosm and microcosm. The triple crown of the hierophant
is bestowed when the lesser and greater worlds are in balance with the self.

UPRIGHT The ability to bridge and connect enables you to make alliances, partnerships and agreements. A respect for tradition, heritage and duty helps you shape your
actions and decisions, ensuring that the spiritual order is respected and not overthrown.
It is time to forgive or to bring reconciliation to warring factions.

REVERSED Iconoclastic and unconventional, your unorthodoxy has overturned things.
Or you may be unable to bypass deeply traditional views to which you hold in blind
faith. Dogmatism and papal pronouncements leave this matter rigidly entrenched and
inflexible. Beware of criticizing or restricting others.

DISCONNECTED Reactive rebellion has exiled you, or pompous attitudes estrange you
from others. Your ideology makes you no more perfect than anyone else. Conventional
attitudes that respect only the mundane world are no help to you. By considering the
spiritual facet of this problem, you will find solution.

VI TWINS

VI TWINS

DIMMI

How do your desires and affinities make a perfect match?
What are the choices offered to you here?

VIRGIN AND CHILD WITH ST ANNE AND THE
INFANT ST JOHN THE BAPTIST

BACKGROUND Leonardo was fascinated with the relationship between Jesus and his cousin, St John the Baptist. There is no biblical warrant for any meeting between the Saviour and his Way-Shower except in the Gospels, where Jesus comes as an adult to be baptized by his cousin, but here Leonardo has chosen to depict the two together as children. (The painting of the left-hand angel in his master Verrocchio's *The Baptism of Christ* was one of Leonardo's first professional tasks.) Apocryphal tradition also suggests an alternative reading of this picture, for it is said that Jesus had other brothers and sisters and that St James, the leader of the early church in Jerusalem after Christ's resurrection, was his brother.

Whichever reading we prefer, here are children who have twin destinies but a unified purpose. Jesus is thrust into prominence to suffer a short life, while St John remains in the shadows, dying in the custody of Herod Agrippa. Separated in life, they are reunited in their shared destiny as lovers of life and wisdom. Leonardo writes, 'The lover is moved by the object of his love, just as the senses are moved by what they perceive: by uniting with the object of his love, lover and beloved become one and the same.' St Anne's upward-pointing finger reminds the children that their destiny is not merely personal but for the love of all creation.

SOUL-CODE Discrimination is a major key to the soul's door. The choices that the soul makes through love and affinity create golden stepping stones along the life-path. The perfect harmony that is established between lovers and friends blesses and consummates your destiny, making life fruitful through tenderness, yearning and trust.

UPRIGHT Attraction and desire draw you into association and partnership. An innate sympathy opens the way to further exchange and possible union. Be sure that you take responsibility for your part of the relationship. Use your knowledge and experience to discern what is being offered to you or what choices you must make now.

REVERSED Poor discrimination leads to messy associations and partnerships which embody neither true love nor purposeful engagement. Conflicts and misunderstandings result from bad choices, and surface affinities may prove to be unfounded. Friends, partners or lovers are incapable of faithfulness or reliability because you are incompatible; separations or splits are likely. Beware of seductive offers.

DISCONNECTED Old partnerships and associations litter the way and make union or commitment difficult. Trust cannot grow overnight, especially after past betrayals, but you can test the waters through small trials. Unless you risk this much you will remain alone. You may be overwhelmed by a dominant partner who is controlling all your choices.

VII IMAGINATION

VII IMAGINATION

DIMMI

Where are you bound? What help brings you through?

A MAN WITH A BURNING GLASS AND
LEGENDARY ANIMALS

BACKGROUND This small but exquisite drawing from the notebooks shows the more mystical Leonardo, who enjoyed fantastic and wonderful creatures. For the reception of King Francis I by Pope Leo X, Leonardo prepared an automaton, a golden lion who walked towards the king and whose breast burst open to show a fleur-de-lys for a heart. In this allegorical image, the man with the burning glass captures the sun's rays, which shine upon a mêlée of fabulous animals, including a serpent-tailed dragon, a unicorn, a lion and a boar who contend together (NOTE: Not all animals are visible on the card image.)

The primary vehicle for Leonardo's ideas and inventions was his imagination. His vision was shaped not only by accurate observation, but also by what his imagination conceived. His whole execution is dependent upon its clear light, which gives power and meaning to what he sees. Through the burning glass of imagination he refracts a multiplicity of images. That he understood and believed so is clear, as he wrote in his notebooks: 'Whatever exists in the universe, whether in essence, appearance or imagination, the painter first conceives it in his mind and then by his hand.' Like the burning glass, which directs and concentrates the sun's beams, imagination powerfully opens the way by conceiving images in the soul that colour our physical sight and understanding.

SOUL-CODE Imagination is the vehicle of your destiny, allowing you to determine the goals and giving you inspiration to attain them. Like a burning glass, the imagination focuses the soul, providing it with maps and clear instructions that will help you achieve your destiny. Maintaining impetus doesn't always mean speed; it is good to note the view as you pass along. Take time periodically to refocus and meditate, reassessing your trajectory. In this way you will keep on track and not lose your way.

UPRIGHT Victory is yours when you focus upon the objective with imagination to help steer you. Movement of projects and the achieving of goals are in your sights. You can overcome obstacles and make progress now if you promote your interests. Travel that helps you relocate or advance is likely. It is important to keep the reins in your own hands and steer your life according to a clear focus. Do not let daydreams draw your chariot.

REVERSED Over-enthusiasm and lack of foresight run you off the road. Things come unstuck, and plans do not succeed due to over-confidence and a failure to fully imagine outcomes. Balance things up and refocus. Trips do not work out satisfactorily, or you become diverted from what you set out to accomplish.

DISCONNECTED Waiting for the right way to rise under your feet only leaves you stationary at the roadside. It is possible you can hitch your plan to a rescue vehicle for a short period only, but the impetus you seek lies within you. Consult and temper your imagination, especially if it is providing you with fearful or fantastic images.

VIII STRENGTH

VIII STRENGTH

VIII STRENGTH

DIMMI

What forces are you bringing into play?
What tendencies need taming here?

A STUDY OF HERAKLES AND THE NEMEAN LION

BACKGROUND Leonardo was surrounded by the *condottieri* (military leaders) of the Italian city-states, hard men of unflinching power like Ludovico Sforza, whose idea of strength was aggression and the merciless overthrow of enemies. This conventional image of strength and capability shows the mythic hero Herakles, who overcomes the Nemean Lion in the first of his twelve labours.

The Nemean Lion was the invincible offspring of the serpent-goddess Echidna and her son, the hound Orthos. Herakles overcame the lion by means of a wrestling match, and not by using his club or sword. He eventually strangled it to death, but was so weary from his labour that he fell into a deep slumber for a month. He finally awoke when the people believed him to be dead, about to sacrifice a ram to honour the dead hero. On his safe return, the ram was then offered to Zeus Soter, or the 'Zeus who Rescues'. Herakles skinned the lion and cut off the creature's claws. In order to honour his semi-divine son, Zeus transported the lion to the heavens, where it became the zodiacal constellation of Leo. Leonardo's ability to tackle his own ambitious labours was based upon a flexibility and an adaptive nature; Herakles with his lion shows how the soul wrestles with life's experience, having to learn the difference between coercion and might, guidance and love.

SOUL-CODE Fortitude and conviction are necessary to follow the soul's destiny to its conclusion. Not everything you meet upon the road is evil, though it may be challenging — or need to be challenged. The ability to tame your instincts and combine them with your strength and compassion brings you to self-knowledge, opening the way to your destiny. The energetic power to hold on and transform matters enables what is wild or unrefined to become cultured and serviceable.

UPRIGHT Courage and patience combined help you face challenges calmly. Your ability to engage with life passionately tempers and matches any wild tendencies or uncontrolled forces. The power of conviction helps you overcome fears. Sexual magnetism attracts others. Strength of mind and a defiant confidence help you wrestle with problems and not be overwhelmed by them.

REVERSED Forcing matters to the conclusion you desire by might alone, or through uncontrolled anger or passion, is inappropriate and self-defeating. An over-zealous approach makes others quail or retreat. You may have bitten off more than you can chew. Your urges and instincts are ruling you more effectively than you are ruling them.

DISCONNECTED You are out of the picture due to a lack of fervour and commitment. A sense of impotence or indifference weakens your position. Onerous connections to dominating people or ideological principles keep you in bondage. Violence or vicious treatment has a stronger hold over you than love. Return to your innate strengths to bring you out of here.

IX HERMIT

IX HERMIT

DIMMI

What light shines in the darkness and solitude?
What shadows does it reveal in this matter?

A CONTEMPLATIVE OLD MAN

BACKGROUND This meditative old man is believed to be a possible self-portrait of
Leonardo done in 1513, in the years before he finally retired to France. Leonardo's
extraordinary career could not have developed without periods of retreat and refresh-
ment. Indeed, the older he became, the less he was interested in social affairs. He
decided to travel to France in 1516, where King Francis I granted him a house of his
own at Cloux, in Amboise in the Loire Valley – the house in which he died in 1519.
Here, the French king visited him often, delighting in the wise variety of his skills and
engaging him in philosophical discussions – possibly to Leonardo's exasperation
with visitors, with whom he could be notably taciturn. At this point, the artist
Leonardo may have been suffering from a partial stroke, which affected the use of one
hand, restricting the amount of work he could do. He writes in his *Treatise on Painting*,
'The painter should be solitary and consider what he sees, discussing it with himself
so that he can select the best parts of whatever he observes. By acting as a mirror
which transmutes itself into as many colours as there are in the objects placed before
him, he will seem to possess a second nature.' The old man in his solitude ponders
the mysteries of life; away from the distractions of popular thought, he discovers the
power of the soul.

SOUL-CODE Introspection and meditation are the tools of self-counsel and knowledge. You go apart to seek the light of the soul and to contemplate the unfolding steps of your destiny. This apparent inaction is an intelligent withdrawal to act as a counterweight and source for fresh action, so that you – and your actions – are informed by the soul.

UPRIGHT Prudent reflection offers you the best way forward. This is not a time or occasion to socialize and be in the centre of things. You need to study or concentrate away from distractions. There may be something that is not yet formulated, and therefore cannot yet be shown or shared.

REVERSED You have turned your back on something, or undue haste has revealed your hand too soon. If it is bad advice you've received, go apart and consider your best action now. Immaturity or the pretence of expertise that you don't possess suggests you need to mature or develop yourself. Relationships have petrified or grown dull.

DISCONNECTED Your shyness or reserve sidelines you, and makes it hard for you to enter into the swing of things again. Too much caution can render you paranoid. Whatever you are trying to hide is also shrouding you from view. Come out into the daylight again and mix with others.

X TIME

X TIME

DIMMI

Where are you moving closer to your destiny?
What opportunities are being offered to you now?

AN ELDER AND YOUTH LOOK AT EACH OTHER

BACKGROUND Age and Youth regard each other over the divide of time: age looking back and youth looking forward. When he was a younger man, Leonardo was recognized by all who saw him as a beautiful youth. With the fading of his beauty and with the mounting physical restraints of old age coming upon him, he repeatedly explored the passage of time. His sketchbooks are full of elderly, toothless men – far more than could ever have been used as models for frescos. His respectful presence at the death-bed of a 100-year-old man who made a good death greatly moved him, obviously revealing something profound about the enigma of time. 'Whatever is beautiful in men is transitory and has no abiding stay.' Paraphrasing Ovid, Leonardo wrote, 'O Time, consumer of everything! O envious age, you destroy and devour everything with the cruel teeth of years, bit by bit, in a slow death.' He quotes the medieval saying, 'When Fortune comes, seize her front with a sure hand, because she is bald behind.' The Roman Goddess Fortuna was believed to be bald, and might only be of service to those who acted swiftly when opportunity presented itself.

Those who lose the moment risk loss or annihilation. Those who are exalted by the opportunity of time can as easily be cast down again. Childless, Leonardo had only his notebooks and paintings to leave to the world at his death. Although he had admirers, he had no true artistic successors in his own time. It is when we are true to the present moment that we are true to the soul.

SOUL-CODE Opportunity, occasion and timeliness are the qualities that combine to bring good fortune. Nothing is fated to the one who lives in the present moment and weighs all things in the light of that moment. This is when destiny is played out – a timeless treasure waiting for you to find it. Though the soul passes through many births, it holds true to promise of its destiny.

UPRIGHT Good fortune is yours if you synchronize with the rhythm being played out. You are part of a wider sequence of events of which this matter is at the hub. Networks spread things further; promotion and opportunity open things up. Things are looking up and coming to culmination.

REVERSED Things are snarled up. Runs of bad luck and missed opportunities make you resentful. Life is unpredictable. If the energy has run out of your plan, you must attend to its rightful time and season, and plant again.

DISCONNECTED Necessity is your master and pins you to a wheel of events that only you can choose to withdraw from. This state of affairs is not fixed, inevitable or forever. Look for the pattern that has trapped you for ways out.

XI EXPERIENCE

XI EXPERIENCE

DIMMI

*How does experience inform your integrity? Where do you
need to be just or impartial in this matter?*

A GIRL POINTS INTO A MYSTERIOUS DISTANCE

BACKGROUND This drawing from the end of Leonardo's life shows an enigmatic pointing girl gesturing into an unknown region, leading us to explore the truth of experience. Calling himself the 'disciple of experience', Leonardo held that experience alone was 'the common mother of all the sciences and arts'. It was in nature and the observation of everyday experience that an artist might learn what everything was about. Those who failed to learn from their direct observation and experience were merely living a lie, in Leonardo's book.

The connection between experience and truth was an intrinsic part of Leonardo's philosophy. In his notebooks, he quoted the adage that 'Truth was always thought to be the only daughter of Time.' He held that 'It is beyond doubt that truth and lies are like light and shadow. Even if it is attached to something small and unnoticed, truth has such an excellence that it surpasses uncertainties and falsehoods about sublime and important matters. Truth will ever remain the chief nourishment of an intelligent mind, though the same cannot be said of a scattered consciousness.' It is the eye of truth and the information of experience that enabled Leonardo to represent his art with such living vibrancy. This mysterious pointing girl shows the way into realms that Leonardo had not yet experienced: the mystery of what lay beyond death. Like a virgin mistress, she encourages him onwards to explore what none has lived to report. The legacy of his life's experience and his championship of truth are the gifts he has left to us.

SOUL-CODE Experience is the arbiter by which the soul's destiny is ruled and balanced. Experience gives the soul a cutting edge to help establish where you are in any given situation. It is through the faculties of perception as well as by the conscience or inner discernment of the soul that the life-path can be walked with integrity, mindful of others who walk alongside. Experience helps you honour your soul's truth.

UPRIGHT Truth will prevail. Balance and equity bring harmony to your project. Honesty and integrity help establish the right of a matter. Your own inner sense of rightness is justified. Things fall in your favour. Agreements, contracts and legal matters base their outcome on your just desserts.

REVERSED Something is deeply unfair, but examine where you have overstepped the mark yourself to find the trigger. A natural bias can result in criticism and undue severity. Legal complications can result, or false accusations that besmirch your honour.

DISCONNECTED Experience has taught you to be tentative or to sit on the fence in this matter. But you cannot remain neutral forever, refusing to engage with life. The ideal state for which you seek has to be laid down by full engagement. A sense of injustice or dishonour keeps you in check.

XII PASSOVER

XII PASSOVER

DIMMI

What are the demands of your destiny? What is being asked of you?

A STUDY OF CHRIST FOR THE
LAST SUPPER FRESCO

BACKGROUND Leonardo completed *The Last Supper* fresco between 1495 and 1498, working at what his patrons felt was a snail-like speed. Each of the models for the twelve disciples had to be found, sketched and painted. He was unable to find a suitable model for Judas for months. His painstaking exactitude suggests a deeper search within himself. Was it possible that he was mindful of what his mentor in mathematics, Luca Pacioli, had written in his book *The Divine Proportion*, a study of the Golden Ratio? Pacioli's book exposited only thirteen 'effects' of the Golden Ratio because, he wrote, 'for the sake of salvation, the list must end'; only thirteen men were present at the table of the Last Supper.

The contemplative Christ seated at the Last Supper knows full well that Judas, the instrument of his destiny, is about to betray him, as he prepares to pass over from life into death for the sake of universal salvation. For Jews, the celebration of the Passover supper marks the liberation of the Israelites from their captivity in Egypt; for Christians, Christ's celebration of this feast marks the occasion where he gives two new commandments: to love one another and to celebrate the Eucharist as an *anamnesis* or remembrance of him. This last moment of his social humanity, surrounded by his disciples, has a poignancy that stretches into timelessness. Poised between life and death, full of realization of his fate, Christ goes within to find the calm authority to surrender and pass over from human into divine existence.

SOUL-CODE Surrender is the soul's method of following the deep vocation of its destiny. The trials and afflictions that challenge you are teachers that reveal the true light that guides you to regeneration. Spiritual turning points are heralded by a confusing mixture of calm and fear. By attending calmly to the moment, by listening to what is being asked of you, a sense of inner guidance can lead you to discover the way.

UPRIGHT You are led to a momentous time of decision in which there seems little real choice. Take a wider view of what is being asked of you. If you look deeper, you will find that it is not sacrifice but consent to a deeper change. It is necessary to give up something in order to gain your desire.

REVERSED A deep unwillingness to let go of your own agenda curtails your opportunities. Preoccupation with fulfilling a fate you have decided on, or been told exists, can leave you suspended between reality and illusion.

DISCONNECTED Prolonged procrastination leaves you feeling stuck or trapped in a situation. Obligations and inconvenient decisions formed in expedience still bind you. Whose destiny are you fulfilling?

XIII DEATH

XIII DEATH

DIMMI

What burdens you or obstructs the way?
What is it that needs to pass in this matter?

CHRIST CROWNED WITH THORNS

BACKGROUND This study of Christ undergoing the humiliation of mockery before death is rare in Leonardo's work. It is notable, in an age of conventional religious art, that he undertook no commission requiring him to paint a Pietà or Crucifixion scene. The nearest he comes to any depiction of Christ's sacrifice is *The Last Supper* and the Christ Child of the *Madonna of the Yarnwinder*, who tenderly reaches towards his mother's spindle with its symbolic cross-piece as if reaching towards his destiny. In his 'prophecies' Leonardo wrote about the sale of crucifixes and other emblems of crucifixion and martyrdom for household display with the air of one intolerant to the perpetuation of images of torture: 'Alas, whom do I see? The Saviour crucified once more.' We can imagine that someone who wrote 'I see Christ sold and crucified once more, and all his saints undergoing martyrdom afresh' did not display such emblems in his own living quarters.

The death of Christ upon the cross is, of course, not a depiction of death as an ending, but as a consummation of the Incarnation and the instrument of death's overthrow. The redemption of mankind through the sufferings of the Saviour who undergoes death, so that it can have no final sting, is the pivot of this picture. In the strange emptiness which lies between the Crucifixion of Good Friday and the Resurrection of Easter Sunday morning, Christ goes down to harrow hell, releasing from bondage all the righteous who have been in a state of expectation. As it says in the Book of Jonah, 'he went down to the peoples of the past'. This realistic realization of death and its ultimate overthrow speaks tellingly of Leonardo's own sense of immortality as well as his faith in the compassion of humanism.

SOUL-CODE Death bids you remember the power of regeneration, without which the soul cannot turn to its destiny. The perpetuation of old cycles hinders the free flow of your life's energies and prevents new growth. The power of decay and elimination come to break down what is overgrown or what is failing to flourish. By allowing the return of life, death is the servant of everything that lives.

UPRIGHT There is a release, dispersal or clarification of things that have been fraught with difficulty. Something has passed and something new can begin. Relief and release make all things new. Things begin to transform, and you are swept into a fresh cycle.

REVERSED There is a resistance to things changing. Stagnation and inertia clog up the works. The sense of threat, trouble or anxiety that is present fails to disperse. By entertaining fear of harm or loss, by pessimistic attitudes, you are only perpetuating the present cycle.

DISCONNECTED You long for release but insist on holding something back, and that is what fails to break the cycle. The place where you've been living feels more like death than life. Return to basics, eliminating what is inessential, and you will find your way through.

XIV TEMPERANCE

XIV TEMPERANCE

DIMMI

How do you balance the opposites that you encounter?
What adjustments are necessary in this matter?

AN ALLEGORY OF THE ERMINE

BACKGROUND The ermine is the name that the stoat is given when it has assumed its white winter coat. Leonardo here portrays the chief mythical attribute of the ermine, which is supposed to be ready to die rather than sully the purity of its white coat. His notebook reads, 'The ermine because of its temperance would rather submit to be captured by hunters rather than seek refuge in a muddy den so that it might not stain its purity.' This allegorical depiction of the Ermine, who would risk death rather than stain her white coat, depicts the Renaissance image of Temperance and self-respect. In one of the earliest Italian tarots to survive the fifteenth century, attributed to Andreas Mantegna, the card of Temperance, one of the seven cardinal virtues, depicts an ermine, emblematic of purity and constancy. In the Mantegna card the ermine peers into a looking glass to inspect its own purity.

Leonardo's own temperance was a by-word among his fellows for, in later life, he became totally vegetarian, a fact so remarkable in carnivorous Italy as to be noted by many. In a letter from Andrea Corsali to Giuliano de' Medici, Corsali writes, 'There are some gentle people called Guzzarati [Gujurati] who refuse to partake of any food with blood in it; they have agreed among themselves to do no harm to any living thing, just like our Leonardo da Vinci.' The ermine of temperance was depicted in one of Leonardo's most striking portraits, that of Cecilia Gallerani, the mistress of Ludovico Sforza, who is shown cradling a tame stoat in her arms. Here the ermine is a punning reference to her name, since *galé* is Greek for 'stoat'.

SOUL-CODE The ability to mediate between opposing states or between the mundane world and the Otherworld is a primary skill which keeps the soul upon the road of destiny. Being neither too full of yourself nor over-humble, you maintain a balance. Transformative changes come about when you begin to skilfully combine outer circumstance with spiritual guidance.

UPRIGHT Moderation and patience combined with discipline and order will help accomplish what you seek. You may have to find the way to reconcile opposites or have to mediate between two extremes in this matter. All that you need is in your hands, if only you can mix, adapt or fuse together what is required. Bearing yourself with modest dignity will not offend others, and will bring balance.

REVERSED Imbalance or excess distort the situation. Opposing elements will not coordinate or mix. Perhaps some things and people cannot come together without mutual loss of self-respect. Communication may be difficult while discord holds sway. You may feel that something is beneath your notice, or it could be you are holding yourself aloof.

DISCONNECTED Disagreements and fallings-out leave you feeling vulnerable or somehow to blame. The dynamics of discord are still spiralling round in you. If self-respect is low, return to your soul's code for encouragement, and return to your innate integrity and taste.

XV PAIN & PLEASURE

XV PAIN & PLEASURE

DIMMI

*What is keeping you in bondage? What is attempting
to dominate you in this matter?*

TWO MEN, CONJOINED FROM THE WAIST

BACKGROUND This extraordinarily curious image occurs in Leonardo's notebooks with the following description: 'Here are pleasure and pain together. They are shown as twins because one is never separate from the other. They are created back to back because they are opposites to each other, existing in the very same body. They share the same foundation, for pleasure's origin is labour with pain, and pain's origins are vain and wanton pleasures. Pleasure is shown with a reed in his right hand to signify uselessness and lack of strength.' His twin is shown with a scourge in his hand, representing pain.

We note that here, again, Leonardo explores the theme of twins, only this pair are the very antithesis of the image found in card VI Twins. The disturbing sado-masochistic overtones of this image of pain and pleasure cannot be ignored. It is possible to discern in Leonardo's words a hint of fastidious self-disgust. The fact that he goes on to write of pleasures taken by the body while in bed which 'fill the imagination with impossible things', and that will 'cause life to fail', speaks of the solitary artist who, out of fear of discovery or intimacy, takes pleasure alone. His early imprisonment on a charge of homosexuality, which could have led to condemnation and death had it been prosecuted with rigour, must have hung over him as a trenchant reminder to be cautious in his sexual encounters. If we take the coin of pleasure, we must pay for it with the whip of pain.

SOUL-CODE The bondage of desires keeps the body subservient and the soul in pain, unable to pursue its destiny. Lack of freedom occurs at the junction where pain and pleasure meet: pleasures spur you on, but their pursuit brings pain and the inability to function or move on. When pleasure is the fulcrum of your life, the free flow of destiny becomes the inexorable wheel of fate to which you are bound by your own desires.

UPRIGHT Limitations, unethical principles or crippling dependencies result from unacknowledged causes. Greed and the poison of in-turned desires affect your performance and dominate your integrity. You seek out what is destructive to you. Projecting blame upon others does not absolve you from cruel behaviour and actions that cause unhappiness.

REVERSED You become free from a bondage that has trapped you in a nightmarish slavery. You have the will and determination to overthrow temptations and tendencies of yourself and others that have led you astray in the past. By casting out fear, you access the power to live with energy and discernment.

DISCONNECTED The sense that others are against you, or are causing your isolation, is not strictly true. Whatever fear causes you aversion also binds you to it. The further you run away, the more likely your isolation will be fuelled by a sense of self-destruction. Re-examine and awaken your self-respect.

XVI DELUGE

XVI DELUGE

DIMMI

What are you shoring up in this situation? What needs to pass?

STORM CLOUDS AND GREAT WAVES
OVERWHELM THE EARTH

BACKGROUND In this study of a tempest, Leonardo explores one of his greatest fas-cinations: the inundations of nature. His interest in the deluges of nature and of Noah's Flood was both geological and theological. He reasoned that if there were deposits of a clearly marine nature embedded deeply at the feet of mountains and hills, then what were the theological implications for the creation of the Earth in six days? This line of reasoning led to potentially controversial areas that might have been regarded as heretical, and so he bent his musings upon the apocalyptic workings of nature instead.

As he grew older, Leonardo's humanism was on less certain ground, as the Church began a movement to counter-reformation. The immoveable authority of the Church had been greatly shaken by the upsurge of Protestantism, and was likely to be less tolerant of what it saw as heretical leanings among scholars and artists. Many of Leonardo's notebooks show drawings of destructive natural forces and catastrophic happenings. He gives lengthy descriptions for such studies, which are to show 'darkness, wind, storms at sea, deluges of rain, forest fires, lightning bolts from heaven, earthquakes, destruction of mountains and levelling of cities'. These accounts relate to actual pictures, in which Leonardo imagines 'What frightful screams were heard in the darkling air, torn apart by the furious thunder and the sudden flashes of lightning breaking through the clouds carrying with them rain that struck down everything in its way.' If there is no temperance in our experience of life, we fall under the effects of what we have unwittingly created.

SOUL-CODE Cleansing change is the instrument by which destiny's pathway is made clear to the soul. This painful scouring action opens the way to illumination, although this may not be immediately apparent when you are dealing with the upheaval or shock. Change comes to break down pride and to clear away an over-dependence upon yourself and your resources.

UPRIGHT Unexpected change, radical shock, or volatile meltdown of something you thought was stable; what feels like utter destruction is actually a catabolic sweeping away of what no longer serves you. Your weaknesses are exposed and you are brought low. Take stock and see how this occasion marks the breakthrough into another phase of your life.

REVERSED The breakthrough or change that has been pending does not arrive. Things are not as you would wish them to be but you make the best of a bad job. During this difficult time you will find it beneficial to work actively to precipitate change by letting go or allowing to pass away whatever is making things stick.

DISCONNECTED If you have been the catalyst for a breakdown, your sense of anger or self-righteousness leaves you in a volatile condition of reaction. Or you may have been on the receiving end of a violent or abrasive encounter where your hurt and pain have caused you to retire from life. Both conditions leave you entrapped in a cycle of recrimination and blame. Return to the root cause of this matter, forgive and move on.

XVII WAY-SHOWER

XVII WAY-SHOWER

DIMMI

*Where are things flowing? What hopeful shoots are
sprouting in this matter?*

ST JOHN THE BAPTIST

BACKGROUND St John the Baptist was the patron saint of Florence, which may partially account for why Leonardo drew and painted him so often, and is still celebrated at midsummer every year, on 24 June (the Feast of the Beheading of St John). The mysterious pointing finger of St John shows the way for all who have wrestled with themselves and overcome the tempest. St John is not the message, only the messenger of the one who will come; he is 'a witness to the light', as it says in the first chapter of St John. He is the 'voice crying in the wilderness' prophesying the coming of one whose shoe he is unworthy to fasten, as he says when he baptizes his cousin Jesus in the River Jordan in a very public acclamation of the Saviour. After St John is imprisoned by Herod at the behest of Herod's wife, John's followers come to him to ask whether Christ is truly the Messiah. He responds that Christ is one who must increase and he, St John, must decrease for the good of the world.

To what degree Leonardo felt himself a forerunner is unknown. So much of what he planned and envisaged predated the time when his ideas could actually be implemented. The ability to envision the effects of our actions ahead of time is like the light of the stars which have taken hundreds of light years to beam upon us: even as they die, so are we illuminated by their rays.

SOUL-CODE Hope is the faith by which your soul journeys towards its destiny. As you learn to follow the signs and messages that give you hope, so you fine-tune to the star of your destiny and allow its gracious beams to fall upon you. Its subtle messages enter your heart and give it new inspiration for the road. After hard times, you can reconsecrate yourself to your destined path with fresh insight and renewed pleasure.

UPRIGHT Hope gives you new heart. The prospect before you is bright with promise. You receive confirmation that you are upon the right path or your inspiration is validated by others. This enables you to dedicate yourself more deeply and bring renewal to situations and relationships that have been ailing. Work naturally and easily with your gifts instead of working against your innate capacities.

REVERSED Inspiration and insight are lacking at this time. Hope seems in short supply, and aspirations very far from being accomplished. You may feel disappointed with yourself, or perhaps you've been behaving like a spoilt diva and have demeaned and offended others through your conduct.

DISCONNECTED You have been pouring out your gifts and talents for those who don't appreciate them. Return to a more balanced approach where you begin to value your gifts and cease to cast them before people who will only abuse and disrespect you. You are worth more than this.

XVIII CONCEPTION

XVIII CONCEPTION

DIMMI

*What do your dreams tell you? What do you intuitively know
about this situation, regardless of appearances?*

LEDA AND THE SWAN EMBRACE, AS THE HUMAN
FRUIT OF THEIR COUPLING EMERGE NEWBORN
FROM EGGS

BACKGROUND The depiction of the Classical myth of Leda's congress with Zeus in the form of a swan marked a distinct break in artistic conventions. Up until the Renaissance, the proper subjects for artists were religious ones. After the fall of Constantinople in 1467, interest in Classical art, learning, architecture and philosophy was stimulated. Instead of looking back to medieval and Christian sources, artists were inspired to explore the Classical roots of Italian culture.

Leonardo made many studies of Leda, perhaps fascinated by the idea of the offspring of human and bird. He wrote of his own memories of being in the cradle when a kite hovered over him and 'opened my mouth with its tail, striking me many times with its wings'. Perhaps this early experience was the source of Leonardo's longing to fly? Looking beyond Christian theology to a more ancient source of illumination, Leonardo writes, 'The moon has no light of its own, but only what it borrows from the sun which illuminates the part that is visible to it.' The conception of Leda's swan-egg children, offspring of Jupiter (Zeus) as Swan, shows what can be conceived when we seek out our immortal destiny.

SOUL-CODE Dreams are the result of the soul overflying the territory through which the path of destiny leads. When you awaken, all you can remember are the symbols, metaphors and ciphers which act as signposts for your way forward. Perceive these calmly and peacefully, without investing them with fearful imaginings or seeing them as fixed and immutable forces that will prosecute your fate. What the soul conceives changes every day, like the moon itself. As it grows, so the way will become clearer and intuition stronger.

UPRIGHT Dreams from the twilight realm generate signs, feelings or apprehensions that make you fearful or confused. The potential of this project is not yet fully realized. Find the rhythm and season of your unique creative arc, rather than rushing the gestation process. The way ahead seems obscure or hidden to you right now, but trust your instincts and travel carefully onward, testing the way.

REVERSED Do not be led into confusion by following the signs dogmatically and literally rather than intuitively. You are not aware of the potentialities of this situation, or you may harbour unrealistic and overblown ideas that bear little relationship to reality. Changes are likely. Do not be drawn into attractive but unstable schemes that promise more than they deliver.

DISCONNECTED You have been deceived or seduced into areas that are unsafe. Or you may feel shamed and exposed by the outcome of a dangerous liaison. As a result, you are submerged in a twilight world of distrust or disgrace where everything and everyone seems out to hurt you. Use every new dawning that it may shine sunlight to disperse the miasma surrounding you.

XIX BIRTH

XIX BIRTH

DIMMI

What light is shining upon you?
What is being born at this moment?

STUDY FOR THE ADORATION OF THE MAGI

BACKGROUND The *Adoration of the Magi* was one of Leonardo's first major commissions. It is inexplicably unfinished, its great promise and originality of treatment incomplete. Here the glorious joy of the *Adoration of the Magi* heralds the birth of Christ as the Sun of Mankind, which was one of the titles by which the Saviour was known (the traditional tarot name for the XIX card is The Sun). Theologians regarded Christ's nativity as like the rising of the sun upon the darkness of ignorance and sin. This was a theme to which Leonardo was drawn many times, though the *Adoration of the Magi* is his most triumphant depiction of birth.

As the ultimate source of light, the sun was for Leonardo his divinity twice over, as he says, 'I will deal with light, exactly as the Lord who is the Light of everything freely enlightens me.' He also wrote, 'The universe's heat and light emanate from the sun', going on to observe, a hundred years before Galileo, that 'the sun does not move'. He noted that 'the sun possesses substance, motion, radiance, heat and the power to generate: all these powers emanate from it without fail'. Bathed in the sunlight of salvation, the soul passes to ultimate illumination.

SOUL-CODE Joy is the natural state of the soul when it is aligned with its destiny. Joy casts a radiance upon the destined path, making the next step easy and light. All things work together to enhance felicity when you take up your unique place in the universe without fear or apology. As you embody the gifts given at your birth, the star of your destiny shines through you. This light can then shine upon those around you, awakening and encouraging those who have lost hope.

UPRIGHT Joy and well-being make you feel young, contented or lucky. You are able to see things from a fresh and optimistic standpoint. Satisfaction and success are yours. You have both the energy and the enthusiasm to see this project through or to shed happiness and enlightenment upon the way of others. Delight in this time of abundant opportunity.

REVERSED The promise of joy you expected has missed the mark. Your sense of pleasure is jaded, or the recognition and success you sought has not been forthcoming to the extent you had hoped. You may feel too exhausted or burned out to enjoy the respite or opportunity offered you now. Relationships that should be happy have fallen into a state of mere mutual toleration.

DISCONNECTED Your pride in achievement has been overshadowed by the successes of others, or your vulnerability arises from broken promises made in good faith. The stain of past experiences colours your self-image and obscures the opportunities of this moment. But all is not dark. Look to the horizon and welcome the joy and illumination that is being freely given to you.

XX RENEWAL

XX RENEWAL

DIMMI

What is awakening? How are you renewed?

A CROWNED EAGLE PERCHES UPON THE GLOBE
OF THE WORLD

BACKGROUND The source of this allegory is unknown, although it has been suggested that Leonardo intended this to represent Pope Leo X as the wolf (which, in the complete picture, is shown in a boat to the left of the eagle) and King Francis I of France as the imperial eagle. This meeting between king and pope was the occasion of Leonardo's retirement from Italy. Francis was so captivated with his genius that he invited him to come and settle permanently in France. In the full image, the wolf in the boat is steering by a compass whose rays connect with those streaming from the eagle's crown, implying that the wolf dances to the will of eagle. But we must also consider Psalm 103, verse 5, which says that '[God] satisfies your age with good things so that your youth is renewed like the eagle.' This verse is based upon a belief that eagles moulted completely every ten years by plunging violently into water to strip off their old plumage. They then had to wait for many weeks to renew their plumage, and so this was a time when they had to trust in God.

This enigmatic allegory suggests another reading: that of the rebirth of belief and culture through the medium of the Renaissance itself, when all things were reconsidered in the light of a complete reappraisal of ancestral and traditional concepts, combining both sacred Christian and aesthetic Classical ideals.

SOUL-CODE The metamorphosis from lifeless body to embodied soul marks the complete cycle of death and rebirth. The changes that are happening reveal a new picture that will affect everything. The crowned eagle, triumphant upon the world, reveals the renewal experienced by the whole world when one soul is true to its destiny. Being faithful to your vocation, you follow the path of destiny with dedication and wonder.

UPRIGHT Transformation is happening. You are awakening to a period of renewal. A message, calling or vocational impulse enables you to sound out your gifts. After a long period of inactivity, silence or obscurity, you can once more strike out in the world by acting, speaking up for yourself and allowing your gifts to shine forth.

REVERSED It is no use trying to resist the changes that are happening here. Although something cherished is being disbanded or dispersed, this is a good time to let the old forms go. When one window closes, a door opens. You can let go of the consequence of poor decisions made in the past if you welcome this change. Do not play for more time, but listen to the deep urging of the soul that guides you to renewal.

DISCONNECTED Exclusion and alienation are barriers that you are maintaining all by yourself as you try to attain retribution or revenge. But as you judge, so shall you be judged. This is the time for forgiveness, in order to sever the shackles of resentment, shame or obligation that have kept you bound. Do not be led astray by dissent and disagreement.

XXI WORLD

XXI WORLD

DIMMI

What is perfected here? How does this matter touch every living part of the macrocosm?

VITRUVIAN MAN IN A SQUARED CIRCLE

BACKGROUND Six centuries ago, on 30 November 1504, when he was 52 years old, Leonardo mysteriously wrote, 'On St Andrew's night I concluded the squaring of the circle.' This observation concerned his lifelong interest in geometric calculations, a study which he undertook in fulfilment of what was written over the door of Plato's Academy: 'Let no one enter here who is ignorant of geometry.' We forget how uneducated Leonardo was, but to keep afloat in a world of culture and learning, he taught himself to geometrize with the best from intense and exact observation.

The classical architect Vitruvius was his mentor when it came to perfect proportion. Quoting him, Leonardo wrote, 'If you decrease your height by one fourteenth by spreading your legs and raising your arms so that your middle fingers are level with the top of your head, your navel will then be the centre of a circle, with your outspread limbs touching the circumference.' The perfectly proportioned Vitruvian Man, with outstretched hands and feet, head erect and proud, encompasses the universe in harmony and freedom. Within the squared circle of the macrocosm, this figure demonstrates how man represents the totality of microcosm, just as Leonardo stretched himself to fulfil the very limits of his destiny. The beggar who began this long journey as the Fool is free from ignorance at last. As Leonardo wrote, 'It is easy to make yourself universal.'

SOUL-CODE Perfection in manifestation is the completion of the soul's destiny. When the macrocosm is perfectly reflected in the microcosm, you know that your life's work is validated in the most magnificent way. There is an ecstatic union between body and soul, a dance of such harmony and wholeness that many are swept into the circle and find the answer of their own inspiration. Not for the self alone does the soul labour, but for the well-being of the whole macrocosm.

UPRIGHT Everything comes to a point of integration, understanding and completion in the most satisfying way. You have come through and triumphed. Now you enter into your freedom without constraint. Your plans arrive at the most favourable point, so act while this opportunity graces you.

REVERSED The lack of response to something that has been completed or achieved is disappointing, but don't take this as a personal affront. The impact has gone deeper and the reaction time will be seen yet. Or you may find that you have not been considering the impact of your plans upon the whole world. Put aside your ego and work for the common good.

DISCONNECTED Your quest for perfection has kept you and your plans on the periphery, outside the charmed circle of success. However, if you will only give up the superiority of pride and the resentment resultant from neglect, you will find acceptance and approval now.

4

MICROCOSM CARDS

THE LESSER MANIFEST WORLD

'Man was rightly called "the microcosm" by the ancients, for man is composed of earth, water, air and fire like the body of the planet itself.'

— LEONARDO DA VINCI

ACE *of* AIR

AIR

ACE *of* AIR
AIR

DIMMI
What are your intentions?

STUDY OF STORM CLOUDS OVER THE SEA

BACKGROUND Leonardo wrote of the air, 'The changeable temperament of the wind is shown by the dust that it raises into the air in gusts and turning eddies ... and by the flags of ships that flutter in different directions.'

SOUL-CODE Clarity of intention is a virtue by which the soul is eternally protected. An alert mind is not confused by the many turnings on the road of destiny, but clearly discerns lies and misleading signals. Truth is a sword in your hand, to protect the vulnerable and keep open the ways of life without fear.

UPRIGHT Clear focus and quick-wittedness help you succeed. Clarity of intention and determination can bring you through. If you assert your rights, you will be irresistible. Whatever your ambition, go for it now.

REVERSED Discriminate and focus upon essentials. Aggression and hostility surround you, but force is not necessarily the answer. Seek the calm clarity of truth rather than the goad of criticism. Ambitions are on hold.

DISCONNECTED Hasty decisions can lead to self-sabotage and ruin things. A lack of boundaries lets in opponents and opportunists. Guard yourself more carefully and connect with the pivot of your will.

TWO *of* AIR RESPECT

TWO *of* AIR

RESPECT

DIMMI
Where is the balance of respect?

SKETCH OF TWO HORSES AND RIDERS

BACKGROUND Leonardo considers the roots of civilization: 'Good culture is the child of a good disposition ... so you must praise a good disposition without culture rather than good culture without the necessary disposition.'

SOUL CODE A balanced, mutual respect makes the way easier for the soul to follow its destiny. You can pursue your path with commitment yet still be mindful of the common well-being of all if you consider both sides. By not trying to trump one another, by according respect to each person's dignity, differences can be worked out.

UPRIGHT Mutual respect can bring peace to a quarrel. Negotiate a truce and suspend hostilities long enough to appraise what the other has to say. Pooling resources enables a non-partisan result for the common good.

REVERSED Partisan feeling or competitiveness unbalances things. Someone is playing on your sympathies, or you want to bring someone you disrespect down. Plans reach stalemate. Peace is unlikely if you discount what others have to say.

DISCONNECTED Ambivalence and indecision arise from feeling disrespected or out of step. You've closed yourself off in order to avoid being influenced. Opponents may not be enemies so much as challengers of your withdrawal.

THREE *of* AIR

TRIALS

THREE *of* AIR
TRIALS

DIMMI

What are you mourning? What is painful?

STUDY OF THE MARTYRDOM OF ST SEBASTIAN

BACKGROUND St Sebastian was martyred under the Emperor Diocletian, who ordered that he be shot to death by arrows. Leonardo wrote of the impact of loss, 'Every trial leaves a sorrow in the memory.'

SOUL-CODE Sorrow tempers the soul by making it face loss and pain. The things that the soul yearns for are sometimes unobtainable or taken away in mysterious ways, but retaliation is not a fitting response. To pursue your destiny, you may find that separation strengthens your concentration, making you more determined to achieve your goal.

UPRIGHT Sorrow results from loss. Trials break to pieces what you are attempting to hold together. Bereavement, heartbreak or separation brings grief; ruptures, quarrels or break-ups bring pain or trouble.

REVERSED Many distractions and confusions disorder your life and make it difficult to concentrate. Old losses still echo in your soul, but you can begin to let them go as new connections form. Beware of retaliation or projecting blame.

DISCONNECTED Divided from what will bring joy, you suffer emotional paralysis. Intensity of loss or longing can bring mental confusion. Do not endure lonely martyrdom but find a friend to witness and help draw out the pain.

FOUR *of* AIR

REPOSE

DIMMI

What rest, space or growing room is needed?

STUDY OF HANDS IN REPOSE

BACKGROUND Some experts believe this study to be intended for a now-lost painting called the *Lady of Lichtenstein*. The protective left hand echoes the universal gesture of a young, newly pregnant mother.

SOUL-CODE Respite after trouble is the opportunity for the soul's clarification and the body's rest. Without periods of repose and healing restoration, following the path of destiny can become merely a treadmill of servitude. During this time apart, remove sources of stress by entering into meditation and observing dreams and thoughts.

UPRIGHT Rest, space or reflection is needed. This is a time for recuperation or an opportunity to attend to your health. Peace and clarity are gained in solitude. Take a retreat from the hurly-burly of life, or a seclusion from work or everyday surroundings.

REVERSED The recovery period is over. It is time to cease from rest and take an interest in your affairs before others do. Exercise caution and economy with your resources or with the expenditure of stamina.

DISCONNECTED The elusive peace that you have sought cannot come without a clearing away of attitudes or connections that have engulfed you in stasis. Winter is over and spring is on the way. Let the dead go.

74

FIVE *of* AIR

CONTENTION

DIMMI
Why, and how, are you trying to be right?

FIVE *of* AIR
CONTENTION

SKETCH OF TWO MEN FIGHTING

BACKGROUND Leonardo's poor opinion of human nature caused him to write bitterly, 'You will see creatures who are always fighting one another with the most terrible losses and frequent deaths on either side.'

SOUL-CODE Contention dishonours and degrades the soul, for it destroys others and obstructs the path of destiny. Antagonism and argument veil a deeper malice, which unconsciously motivates many of our actions. Always having to be right diminishes the other person.

UPRIGHT Contention and trouble are likely. Someone tries to take advantage or usurp your position. Unethical tactics and dirty tricks keep you on alert. You win a fight, but victory is so hard-won that it's barely been worth it. Insistence upon your own way triggers arguments.

REVERSED Uncertainty dogs your steps. Treachery is in the air. Attempts at reconciliation meet little mutual agreement. Dig deeper to find out what has been buried out of sight, because it will change everything. Check motivations carefully.

DISCONNECTED Your deeply held beliefs are not shared by others. Examine the practical application of your views, as they may be too abstract. Your sense of dishonour can be healed by someone apologizing, or by putting things behind you.

SIX *of* AIR

FLOWERING

DIMMI
Which beliefs and attitudes support or block you?

STUDY OF VIOLETS

BACKGROUND This study of violets is one of Leonardo's many botanical drawings. Considering his restless, peripatetic life, he asks, 'Where shall I take my place? In a while from now, you will know.'

SOUL-CODE The ability to distance yourself from dangers or to seek new perspectives from a neutral standpoint helps the soul evaluate what needs to change. The path to destiny can be blocked by old beliefs, ideas and attitudes, or diverted into ever-narrower dead ends. The violet always finds a secret place to flower in safety.

UPRIGHT You breathe more easily as dangers fall behind you. You find a new way over and through, or you distance yourself from dangers. Decide which resources or attitudes still serve you, and take them with you.

REVERSED Delays stalemate you. Something needs to change or be disclosed for the present situation to move forward. Look closer at the options offered to you. Review prejudices and examine old beliefs.

DISCONNECTED Dealing with things expediently means you hardly affect present conditions. By avoiding difficulty you continue to be hedged around with indecision. Plan a change or an escape route.

SEVEN *of* AIR

ACTION

SEVEN *of* AIR
ACTION

DIMMI
What action needs taking?

STUDY OF THE CHRIST CHILD

BACKGROUND Leonardo's notebooks refer to an unknown incident with a powerful patron: 'When I portrayed a Christ Child, you imprisoned me. If I show him grown up, will you do worse to me?' It may refer to his arrest for homosexuality in 1476.

SOUL-CODE Action is born of new ideas and intentions, becoming the vehicle for the soul's experience. The hope that underlies your endeavour brings confidence to the path of destiny. The body's actions help manifest the soul's intentions. When the two are united, there is a sense of glorious strength.

UPRIGHT New endeavours bring hope and confidence. The active working-out of your desires helps compensate for old losses, or recoups something you thought long vanished. Have faith in your actions and stand firm.

REVERSED You have to be careful you're not caught. You may be downplaying shameful behaviour or suffering a crisis of confidence. Someone's advice keeps you from taking action, or perhaps you are being over-cautious.

DISCONNECTED You attempt to retrieve something precious and make it work now, but the power has gone out of it. Agonizing over personal mistakes places you in the past. It is time to move into the present.

EIGHT *of* AIR

CONFINEMENT

DIMMI

What bypasses the limitations surrounding you?

MAN IN VERTICAL FLYING MACHINE

BACKGROUND Leonardo was obsessed with the aerodynamics of flight: 'The man in a flying machine must be free ... It is as well not to be confined by iron bands but with harness of leather and silk cord rigging.'

SOUL-CODE When the soul is in a narrow place, it has to return to the core directive of its destiny, flying over the possibilities that lead from restraints and limitations. Such initiatory tests help to hone determination, as well as showing you where you must stand and endure.

UPRIGHT Things come to a crisis where you will need to be flexibile. But in all this conflict and turmoil you are restrained by conventions, self-beliefs or obligations imposed upon you. Calm ingenuity is your best friend now.

REVERSED You are in a position to cut the Gordian knot of the present impasse. Hard work and its resultant difficulties can be lightened by lateral thinking or unconventional means. Improvise your way through the restraints.

DISCONNECTED Adverse criticism has undermined you, or you may be harbouring self-beliefs that keep you bound in a narrow place. By becoming isolated from sources of help you are courting a sense of victimhood. Shout for help and listen to advice.

NINE *of* AIR

NINE *of* AIR
DANGER

DANGER

DIMMI
What do you fear? Do you flee or fight?

MASSIVE CANNONS DISCHARGE SHOT

BACKGROUND Leonardo's scientific interest in propulsion outstrips considerations of what cannons can do: 'Observe how long a stone discharged from a cannon maintains its movement.' But he also observes, 'He who fears dangers doesn't perish by them.'

SOUL-CODE Fear is poison to the soul. The way to keep travelling along destiny's road while subjected to severe anxiety and danger is to keep focused upon the power that sustains your life. When matters come to fight or flight, the need to survive must be weighed against the likelihood of injury. There is no shame in avoiding danger, but some situations require searching sacrifices.

UPRIGHT Anxieties and dangers beset you. Concern keeps you wakeful. Past events and slights circle in your mind, colouring everything else. Be cautious, but do not allow fear to overwhelm or petrify you.

REVERSED Fear and depression are passing. You receive encouragement to help you back on your feet again. Reasonable fears may be founded in reality. Attend to your doubts and scruples without delay.

DISCONNECTED Irrational fears and morbid fantasies nest in your soul. Exorcize these by exploring their origin, exposing them to the light of day, where they will wither. Seek psychological help or healing.

TEN *of* AIR

PUNISHMENT

DIMMI
What do you have to relinquish?

THE HANGED BODY OF AN ASSASSIN

BACKGROUND In April 1478, the brother of Lorenzo de' Medici was brutally assassinated. One assassin, Bernardo di Bandino, escaped and hid, but was captured and hung from the Bargello for all to see.

SOUL-CODE The soul is subjected to disintegration and surrender in order to renew whatever has lost its purpose. When anyone's life-path has trespassed against the integrity of destiny, there is always a just balancing-up. When the promise and contract of life itself is broken, then the vehicle of life itself shatters to let out the poison.

UPRIGHT There is pain and disappointment. Things come to crisis and an ending. The struggle is over, or else is useless; it is time to let go of whatever will not come again. The trouble you have sown begins to manifest.

REVERSED Things get better. You have survived and come through. The stressful pace begins to slow up. The constraints that have been put upon you are released.

DISCONNECTED What story are you telling against yourself? You are imprisoned by self-pity and acceptance of blame. It is time to transform the old story and explore new possibilities.

PAGE *of* AIR

PAGE *of* AIR

DIMMI

What do you have to watch out for?

SKETCH OF A YOUTH

BACKGROUND This swiftly executed sketch of a young man could represent one of the many apprentices who prepared Leonardo's pigments, cleaned his studio and learned the principles of an artist's craft.

SOUL-CODE Vigilance is the servant of the soul, enabling you to travel safely upon the path of destiny. Whatever trials and challenges lie in wait, you will be prepared to face them and deal with them, using your physical agility and mental cunning. By observing all the approaches, you are a servant of the sanctity of life itself.

UPRIGHT Insight and vigilance help you discover what is hidden. Some strategizing is necessary. Keep your wits about you and remain agile; you may need to improvise at short notice. There may be news about negotiations or contracts.

REVERSED You back down in the face of forceful opposition, rather than standing your ground. Use mental dexterity and repartee to prevent you from feeling weak and powerless. Unforeseen difficulties arise. Someone has you under surveillance.

DISCONNECTED Defensiveness or suspicion keep you at arm's length from the action. Hurtful gossip or the compulsion to argue make socializing difficult. You feel vulnerable or exposed. Better preparation will help you.

KNIGHT *of* AIR

KNIGHT *of* AIR

DIMMI

What must you champion or defend?

SKETCH OF A MAN ON A REARING HORSE

BACKGROUND This execution of a warrior overcoming his enemy was intended for the monument to Leonardo's patron, Ludovico Sforza. Leonardo writes, 'He who refuses to punish evil permits it to be done.'

SOUL-CODE Championship of high ideals is a noble task, for the soul is armoured as much as the body. The warrior who wields a sword to defend or a tongue that argues for others is in charge of a potentially wounding weapon. Your high-minded defence of the weak protects the core principles by which life is lived.

UPRIGHT Courage and skill are your hallmarks. You are used to cutting a dash and being first in the fray. But don't be so sharp that you cut yourself – or others. Something needs to be rescued, or an idea or plan needs your support.

REVERSED Avoid vengeful retaliation. Life isn't about getting even. Impatience and fanaticism can render you incapable and delusional. Sharp words and blame must be controlled.

DISCONNECTED Your ideas have run away with you, and are dragging you behind them. Alternatively, you are charging ahead regardless of advice to the contrary. As the victim of an injustice you may seek retreat rather than restitution.

LADY *of* AIR

LADY *of* AIR

DIMMI
What is really going on?

STUDY OF A WOMAN IN A CAP

BACKGROUND Leonardo drew this unknown young woman between 1485 and 1490. She may be a married woman or a servant. He writes, 'It seems no small thing for a painter to give a pleasing grace to his subjects.'

SOUL-CODE Discrimination is a hard-won quality that arises from the experiences of walking the path of destiny. The knocks, losses and disappointments of life give you a true eye and enable you to deal with things efficiently. As a shrewd judge and honest guardian of independence, you are a mother of life who speaks as a friend.

UPRIGHT Use your shrewd perception to see into the heart of things. Offer your guidance or judgement. Draw upon your past difficult experiences to make things better, rather than to transmit any pain to the present.

REVERSED Your keen perceptions and quick words can cause hurt and offence; don't allow criticism and censure to replace compassion. Self-deception and sorrow can make you too hard on yourself. Set some limits.

DISCONNECTED Seeing things from your perspective of loss is poisoning everything. This bitterness encourages you to wallow in grief. The longer you separate yourself, the more you will be motivated by anger and retaliation.

LORD *of* AIR

LORD *of* AIR

DIMMI

How must you temper power with fairness?

STUDY OF CESARE BORGIA

BACKGROUND The illegitimate son of Pope Alexander VI, Cesare was a brilliant soldier and a ruthless manipulator whose motto was 'Aut Caesar, aut nihil' – 'Caesar or nothing'. Leonardo served him in 1502.

SOUL-CODE Scrupulous attention to detail and disciplined logic give shape to life's disorders and muddles. The power to command the soul's path lies in your hands, as long as you keep focused upon your destiny in an intelligent way. But an inability to empathize can change power into ruthless, dictatorial cruelty. When you lead others justly, you are a father of all life.

UPRIGHT Evaluate things with power and authority; reason helps you see what is fair and just. Attend to matters of principle. Use your critical and discerning eye carefully. Cut losses by making sacrifices.

REVERSED Over-discipline or a ruthless expediency constrains you or others. Having no mercy for yourself, you offer none to anyone else. Be careful whom you put down, or they might be crushed. Read the small print carefully.

DISCONNECTED Disillusionment in the system and fear of corruption or injustice makes you hide away or put yourself beyond the law. At odds with your own authority, you cannot honour yourself until you claim it back again.

ACE *of* FIRE

FIRE

DIMMI
What creative plan are you beginning?

ACE *of* FIRE
FIRE

A STUDY OF ROCKS EXPLODING

BACKGROUND Leonardo wrote, 'Fire destroys lies and deceptions, restoring truth and casting out darkness. It is the light, banisher of the darkness that conceals all essential things.'

SOUL-CODE Creative passion is the soul's way of kindling enthusiasm and energy for the manifestation of destiny's gifts. This sacred torch lights the way when all seems dark, its beams dispelling doubt and false observation. The gift of creativity is a command to live and engage to the best of your ability.

UPRIGHT There is a great deal of creative energy. From a fortunate beginning a new project can flourish. The conception of an idea is rapidly followed by opportunities to develop and manifest it. There is a magic in the air and a sense of enterprising adventure.

REVERSED Enthusiasm without due preparation leads you to jump the gun, resulting in a false start or premature beginning. Your ideas currently outstrip your capacity. Spend more time at the drawing board.

DISCONNECTED Being unable to get started, your ideas and dreams can't manifest. You are turned down and unable to get going again. Do not grow resigned to this detachment, for the energy that powers your ideas also fuels your life.

TWO *of* FIRE

DIRECTION

DIMMI
What is attained here?

THE EMBLEM OF A COMPASS FIXED TO A STAR

BACKGROUND This emblem is described as 'an unwavering course', accompanied by the words, 'whoever is fixed to this star will not revolve'. The sense of this is that the bearer of this emblem will not be troubled if he holds his course.

SOUL-CODE Maturity of soul grows through trust in the destined path, and by fostering the gifts you've been given. When the energy and light of your star of destiny shines upon you, the way is revealed and hidden doorways open to usher you into new opportunity. Winds may veer, pathways may become unclear, but the needle points to your destination.

UPRIGHT You have the ability to attain your ideals if you are brave enough to follow where they lead. Your maturity of outlook gives life a distinctive style and influence. Ventures merit expansion.

REVERSED Something surprising is in the wings. Things may utterly transform themselves, or else meet a dead end. Over-ambitious ideas, or undue pride in your attainments, can humble you.

DISCONNECTED You feel beholden or in awe of those more powerful than yourself. Feeling unworthy means that you need to reconnect with the gifts you undoubtedly possess. Follow the current crop of opportunities.

THREE *of* FIRE

MATRIX

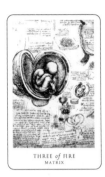

THREE *of* FIRE
MATRIX

DIMMI

What have you conceived? What is ready to be born?

A FOETUS IN THE WOMB

BACKGROUND Leonardo's anatomical dissections yielded this extraordinary image of an unborn child. He concluded, 'The same soul governs these two bodies, sharing the desires, fears and sorrows with this creature.'

SOUL-CODE The soul pursues a risky enterprise when it takes a body to be its vehicle. From the fragile beginnings of conception and birth to the final steps upon the destined path, it takes courage and vision. You cannot ensure that things will turn out the way you hoped, but the patient trust you learned in the womb will sustain you.

UPRIGHT Initiative and acumen launch your endeavours, while good connections help maintain your creative output. Your enterprise needs courage and daring. The way in which your plans are received is not in your hands.

REVERSED Beware of accepting help from someone with ulterior motives. Ensure that over-dependence upon your connections doesn't lead to you taking them for granted. Exercise foresight and caution. Plans miscarry.

DISCONNECTED Feeling sidelined by your own lack of enterprise and adventure, you look on with growing bewilderment while others promote themselves. It is time for your creative ideas to be born.

FOUR *of* FIRE

CELEBRATION

DIMMI

What is the cause for celebration?

SKETCH OF MUSES OR GRACES DANCING

BACKGROUND Leonardo was also a musician, and played the lyre, or *lyra de braccio*. Of music he writes, 'The graces of the body may be observed in a variety of harmonic rhythms which, in dying and being born, delight the soul of man.'

SOUL-CODE Celebration is a sacred duty for the soul, and enables the path of destiny to be blessed by gladness and the company of friends. Ritual and seasonal celebrations are not for your benefit alone, but are times when the gods may be invited to earth to partake in the good things you enjoy.

UPRIGHT Prosperity allows you to share the rewards with others. Relationships flourish and reunions give pleasure. Seasonal enjoyment and celebration help you relax. Enjoy leisure and sacred celebration.

REVERSED Your project's early promise has not paid off. Insecurity dogs your steps. Relationships don't work out. Social gatherings don't yield full enjoyment, for something is missing. Your happy leisure time is over.

DISCONNECTED Even though everyone around you is enjoying themselves, you feel outside the charmed circle of acquaintance. Social engagements make you morose, shy or gauche. Arrange a rite of passage that brings you out.

FIVE *of* FIRE

STRUGGLE

FIVE *of* FIRE
STRUGGLE

DIMMI

What strategies are necessary to settle this conflict?

SKETCH OF A BATTLE SCENE

BACKGROUND The various battles for supremacy among the Italian city-states made Leonardo's life subject to great disruption. He depicted many battles, including the lost fresco of the Battle of Anghiari.

SOUL-CODE Conflicts cannot be avoided on the path of destiny. Struggles to assert the space that your soul must take up are necessary, or you will be overset and abused. By exploring the many possibilities, and by using humour and decisive strategies, you clear the road ahead of you. The disputes that cannot be settled must go to arbitration for judgement.

UPRIGHT There is competition, and you have to struggle to maintain your position. Ingenuity is your most important weapon in this conflict. Those who work with you may need acknowledgement, or animosity may develop.

REVERSED Disputes and litigation are likely. Complexities arise on a current project. Things have shifted due to sabotage or insider-dealing. Persecution and harassment make you feel conflicted.

DISCONNECTED When things get difficult, you pull in your horns and hide. Sibling rivalries, peer pressures or conflicts at work exhaust and confuse you. The way through is not to take sides but to calmly maintain your neutrality.

SIX *of* FIRE

VICTORY

DIMMI
What has been achieved or realized?

STUDY OF THE TRIVULZIO MONUMENT

BACKGROUND The triumph of the Italian mercenary Gian Giacomo Trivulzio, who captured Milan on behalf of the French army, was to have been celebrated by this monument, but the French were expelled and the work discontinued.

SOUL-CODE The enjoyable triumph of victory should not obscure the fact that this is but one battle in a longer struggle to win through to your destiny *and* stay on course with it. But the realization of hopes and desires encourages the soul nevertheless. Beware of standing upon a pedestal or of glorying in the defeat of others.

UPRIGHT Whether it is a great triumph or just good news, you are through to a place of gain and realized desire. The reward for your efforts is the sense of a job well done. Self-empowerment and advancement are yours.

REVERSED Your victory is short-lived. Pride goes before a fall. Leadership is needed now to help rescue matters. Everything is delayed and put off again. If this goes on, rewards will be negligible.

DISCONNECTED Fear of success is a drag on your soul's trajectory. You may be resisting the limelight or retiring from work earlier than you need. If others are pulling you down, it may be time to change horses.

SEVEN *of* FIRE

SUCCESS

DIMMI

What's in your favour? Where must you back down?

SEVEN *of* FIRE
SUCCESS

STUDY OF A NAKED MAN WITH BEASTS

BACKGROUND This vigorous study is related to the story of Herakles and the Nemean Lion, like the card of VIII Strength. The results of Leonardo's anatomical studies are clear from his treatment of the musculature.

SOUL-CODE Overcoming obstacles is a continual task for the soul. The path to destiny is not walked without rivalries, problems and confrontations. Success sometimes comes at the price of loss of stamina or the alienation of supporters who disagree or are jealous. It is not possible to keep the advantage forever without becoming aggressive.

UPRIGHT Gain and success are likely. Although obstacles and challenges seem overwhelming, you have the advantage. Keeping the upper hand in discussions or negotiations, you have to draw on all your ingenuity.

REVERSED Hesitation through embarrassment or indecision causes loss. Defensive barriers keep you at bay. You may feel uneasy or caught on the hop; if you vacillate, others will crowd in and take over.

DISCONNECTED The obstacles seem too great and your doubts are invading your capacity. You cannot retain your popularity with everyone if you remain sitting on the fence. Act decisively, even if it means making a few enemies.

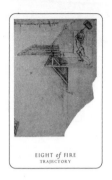

EIGHT *of* FIRE

TRAJECTORY

DIMMI

Where are you aiming your intentions?

PLAN OF A MULTIPLE-CATAPULT DEVICE

BACKGROUND This drawing is one of Leonardo's many designs for cutting-edge military efficiency. This multiple catapult with rapid-assault capability remained on the drawing board.

SOUL-CODE The trajectory of the soul's path is discovered by energetic enthusiasm and keen perception, enabling swift progress. Your destiny can, however, easily be overshot through poor observation and unformed enthusiasm, leaving you to collect the arrows of your unstable desires from the petty undergrowth of life. Demarcate your way by regarding the signs and synchronicities that come to you.

UPRIGHT Rapid progress is being made, and quick decision-making may be needed. There is plenty of enthusiasm and energy for what you want to do, but beware that you don't act too hastily. Don't overestimate your resources.

REVERSED Things are spinning out of control and effort is wasted. Your rapid advancement can be the cause of envy. Quarrels and disputes spring up. Gossip injures reputations larger than yours.

DISCONNECTED The limitations that have hemmed you in have been suddenly removed, but internal doubts cause delay, leading to further stagnation. It is time to get moving again – but aim carefully.

NINE *of* FIRE

REPELLING

NINE *of* FIRE
REPELLING

DIMMI

What trouble are you expecting? How can you deal with it?

DESIGN FOR A METHOD OF REPELLING
SIEGE LADDERS

BACKGROUND Given the perilous times in which Leonardo lived, this simple device, which raises a set of battens to repel siege ladders, would have been welcomed as a practical defence by the warring city-states.

SOUL-CODE The soul must remain vigilant if there are expectations of trouble ahead. Mature risk assessment and proper caution help clear the path of destiny, so that you don't become overwhelmed by an unrealistic sense of danger or a sense of inadequacy. Resourcefulness and conviction are the guards who repel your opponents.

UPRIGHT Difficulties and troubles lie ahead, but you have time to prepare defences. Discipline and clear planning are called for. Assess the risks. Plans are under attack; draw upon deep or accumulated resources.

REVERSED Obstacles and problems keep fouling your operation. These troubles may be trivial but their impact is affecting your health and outlook. Pay attention to nagging instincts. Continual attrition weakens you.

DISCONNECTED The continual welter of daily life makes you lose sight of the main objective. You are losing the wood for the trees. Re-evaluate your motivations: do you need to struggle on, or to change tack?

TEN *of* FIRE

BURDENS

DIMMI

What is weighing you down?

A HUGE CANNON IS HOISTED BY A CRANE

BACKGROUND This massive cannon being laboriously hoisted is one of Leonardo's military engineering drawings for Ludovico Sforza. Men labour like ants in this arsenal of destructive weaponry.

SOUL-CODE Responsibilities and obligations cannot be laid aside lightly when you have entered into a contract. It is wise to weigh the unseen cost of agreements if the soul is not to become burdened and deflected from the path of destiny. Ensure that you are capable of the task, or renegotiate the contracts you have taken on.

UPRIGHT Excessive pressures burden you, and deadlines bring things to crisis. Obligations and expectations weigh heavily, and you are loaded with crushing respon-sibilities. Projects have become onerous. You shoulder burdens out of pride.

REVERSED Delegate your responsibilities or relinquish them. Results do not justify your efforts. It may be time to move on, downsize or declutter. You have to justify and defend your reputation when you come under attack.

DISCONNECTED You have been left supporting a burdensome task, or someone has passed the buck onto you. A sense of overload or burnout weighs you down. These tasks sideline your true worth and natural skills.

PAGE *of* FIRE

PAGE *of* FIRE

DIMMI

What kindles your enthusiasm or passion?

STUDY OF ST JAMES THE ELDER FOR
THE LAST SUPPER

BACKGROUND St James was the disciple who witnessed the Transfiguration of Christ. He and his brother John were called 'sons of thunder' for wanting to call heavenly fire upon the Samaritans who ignored Christ's message.

SOUL-CODE The soul's ardent fervour lends fire and enthusiasm to every step of the unfolding path of destiny. When this fervour is ignited, passion makes the necessary connections between desire and fulfilment. As the servant of idealism, beware that your torch does not scorch others.

UPRIGHT You have the enthusiasm to pursue your dream. Your frank, resourceful and reliable capacity creates fresh opportunity. A sense of adventure acts as a catalyst for change. News opens up another avenue.

REVERSED You feel lacking in enthusiasm and drive. Irresponsible and immature actions put plans at risk. Indecision and instability make you reluctant to stir. Take gossip with a pinch of salt.

DISCONNECTED Shocking news has arrested your life. You or others have acted delinquently and have been warned. It is childish to nurse your wounds and hide away. Be more discriminating, and learn from your mistakes.

KNIGHT *of* FIRE

KNIGHT *of* FIRE

DIMMI

Where are you called to be adventurous?

STUDY FOR A TRIUMPHAL ARCH

BACKGROUND This proposed triumphal arch was intended to celebrate the capture of Milan by Gian Giacomo Trivulzio, who led the French army, but the commission was never executed.

SOUL-CODE The spirit of adventure brings light into manifestation. The unpredictability of the soul's path is no obstacle to the light-bringer who scouts for the signs of destiny. The energy of the trickster both prepares and helps reassure those who loiter at the passes to the new country ahead of them, guarding and enabling their transition into the unknown.

UPRIGHT You are a fearless adventurer who plunges into the unknown. You initiate more than you will commit to. Explore revolutionary ways of tackling problems spontaneously. Transplant, move on or relocate.

REVERSED Impatience and recklessness cause disruption and break-up. You are simmering with rebellion, or on the verge of losing your temper. Try to tackle things more slowly and patiently, so that you are not seen as a hustler or bully.

DISCONNECTED You have chosen not to absent yourself from the adventure of your life, which may have felt like a foreign place till now. Use this opportunity to pass into the place prepared for you, and be exiled no longer.

LADY *of* FIRE

LADY *of* FIRE

DIMMI

How can you manifest your passion in a practical way?

STUDY FOR THE LOST PAINTING,
LEDA AND THE SWAN

BACKGROUND Italian prostitutes assumed this complex braiding. This drawing may show La Cremona, mistress of Giacomo Alfei in Milan. She is listed among Leonardo's entourage in 1509; whether as mistress or merely model is not known.

SOUL-CODE Radiance emanates from the soul when self-confidence is ignited. When this radiant light warms others with sincere friendship, you become a mother of light, ensuring companionship upon the destined path and easing the discomfort of the guest to life's banquet. Passionate beliefs combine with a ready grace to bring energy, determination and stability to the vagaries of life.

UPRIGHT Passionate, warm and loving, you desire to oversee and organize things from centre stage. Ardent and friendly, you can afford to be sympathetic and gracious. There is an enterprising energy available to you.

REVERSED Your dynamism may be too strong, your passion too explosive. The need to control, over-dramatize or be confrontational is exhausting others. Envy or jealousy makes the situation volatile.

DISCONNECTED A sense of obligation binds your independence. A perceived need to dance attendance, nurse or foster others puts you in the shade. Someone wants you kept in place, but it is time to assert your rights.

LORD *of* FIRE

DIMMI

How are your magnanimity and courage needed?

STUDY OF ST BARTHOLOMEW FOR
THE LAST SUPPER

BACKGROUND As Christ utters the words, 'One of you will betray me,' at the Last Supper, St Bartholomew leans forward in consternation, though from the concern in his intelligent face these words clearly don't apply to him.

SOUL-CODE Magnanimity ennobles the soul, giving the dignity and courage to explore the fullest extent of the destined path. Self-respect and honesty maintain your achievement, but don't become overbearing or egotistical. When the benevolent light that you shed encourages pride, dignity and self-respect in the hearts of those who are dependent or unenlightened, you are a father of light.

UPRIGHT A strong, devoted honesty brings vital self-assurance to whatever is unfolding. You can act as a creative entrepreneur or mentor and afford to be magnanimous or lend support to those less fortunate around you.

REVERSED Autocracy and dogmatism only leads to self-righteousness or loss of dignity. People look to you for example, and are disappointed. Delegate some of your tasks to others; it won't weaken your position.

DISCONNECTED Fear of someone leads you into appeasement as a means of control. This uneasy game of tyrant and victim leads only to weakness and further abuse. Use your creative intelligence to leave this servitude.

ACE *of* WATER

WATER

ACE *of* WATER
WATER

DIMMI

What is irrigated or blocked?

WATER FALLS INTO A HOLLOW

BACKGROUND Leonardo was fascinated by water, serving as an overseer of waterways. He noted that 'The water that you touch in a river is the last of what has passed by and the first of whatever comes.'

SOUL-CODE The ability to follow the flow of destiny's path brings the soul a sense of fulfilment and nurture. Love blesses all enterprises that you undertake when you find the flow of the current that impels you. A state of deep reflection further nourishes your dreams, opening you up to intuitive messages.

UPRIGHT Abundance and fertility are possible. Beauty and pleasure walk with you. You are deeply nurtured by aesthetic harmony. Love makes all things new. Generosity opens its hand.

REVERSED Looking within for the source of pleasure and harmony, you become self-centred. Access to deep intuition is blocked. You feel eroded, sterile and unstable. Step back into the stream with a more generous spirit by finding the rhythm of the flow.

DISCONNECTED Emotional deprivation makes you fear beauty, and so you assume a brash exterior that fools no one. Seek the nurture of beauty in all its forms and learn to love again.

TWO *of* WATER

UNION

TWO *of* WATER
UNION

DIMMI
What brings unity or reciprocation?

AN ANATOMIC CROSS-SECTION OF A MAN AND WOMAN ENGAGED IN COITUS

BACKGROUND Leonardo writes, 'A man wants to know if a woman is amenable to his desires. Perceiving that his desire is reciprocated, he makes his request and puts his desires into action.'

SOUL-CODE Union with another soul strengthens the will to live and brings harmony to the soul. When differences are transcended in brief moments of unity, a sense of deep peace and concord with the whole universe is experienced. Microcosm and macrocosm meet and mate in such sacred moments of oneness.

UPRIGHT You will find reciprocation in friendship or passion in partnership. The meeting of hearts and minds makes love not only viable but also productive, as two come together to love or plan. In fusion, peace and harmony prevail.

REVERSED The differences between you and a friend or partner are wrong-footing the relationship. Misunderstandings arise, threatening separation and estrangement. Thwarted desires and plans bring trouble, quarrels or disunity.

DISCONNECTED You have disengaged or been too laid-back, giving the wrong impression. More reciprocation in your relationships will deepen your friendships and bring intimacy to your partnerships. Stress similarities rather than differences.

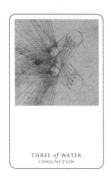

THREE of WATER
CONJUNCTION

THREE *of* WATER

CONJUNCTION

DIMMI
What is coming together?

THREE *of* WATER
CONJUNCTION

THE LIGHT OF PLANETARY BODIES CONVERGES

BACKGROUND Leonardo's studies of optics, light refraction and astronomy meet in this diagram showing how the light of two luminous and two opaque bodies converges to form pyramids of light.

SOUL-CODE The conjunction of like-minded friends or the convergence of supportive circumstances encourages the soul. The relief of shared ideas and the mutuality of peers helps your path of destiny appear in sharper focus. The enjoyment you experience when things come together in one bond makes life worth living. Healing and solace come from alliances and coincidences, providing resolution and a happy ending.

UPRIGHT There is healing and resolution. Alliances work well and friends gather in fulfilment. Difficulties come to an end. You are blessed with happy coincidences, serendipity and congenial assemblies, and experience mutual support and sharing.

REVERSED Dissipation and excess cause fracture and delay, or too many commitments mean no social time or relaxation. It is hard to get people together, or there is no cooperation possible.

DISCONNECTED You don't mix with your peers or are at odds with the merry-go-round. Exclusion from the group collective is hard. You have changed, and can't appreciate old pleasures. Find new friends who share your interests.

FOUR *of* WATER

DISAPPOINTMENT

DIMMI
Where have desires outstripped expectation?

FOUR *of* WATER
DISAPPOINTMENT

MOULD FOR THE SFORZA HORSE

BACKGROUND Leonardo ambitiously attempted to mould the greatest statue ever cast in metal for his patron, Ludovico Sforza. His lack of technical expertise made it impossible: 'We all know that mistakes are more easy to recognize in the works of others than in our own. By criticizing the mistakes of others we may ignore greater ones that we have made.'

SOUL-CODE The ability to assess errors that are made upon the way helps redefine the path of the soul's destiny when it has strayed into unfruitful lines. Withdraw without blame as the old path falls away, and look for fresh signposts.

UPRIGHT Motivation has run out. Disappointment or weariness makes every experience bitter. There is a sense that you are only time-serving in this situation, or that time has stopped. Rethink your plans or recover from the illusion where fancy has led you.

REVERSED Fresh possibilities arise from an unexpected quarter. New associations and friends bring you out of a period of stalemate. The discontent you experience is the stir of creative change.

DISCONNECTED You are brooding on failure, or are caught up in a fantasy world. Old experiences colour everything you do: you are wound in them as in a net. Let this old stuff go.

FIVE *of* WATER

UNWINDING

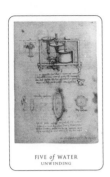

FIVE *of* WATER
UNWINDING

DIMMI

What old patterns cause present loss? What new designs clear the way?

MECHANISM TO EQUALIZE AN UNWINDING SPRING

BACKGROUND This is one of Leonardo's many mechanical drawings that explore impetus, movement and power. 'I ask in which part of its circular motion will the cause that moves it leave the thing moved or moveable?'

SOUL-CODE Loss of impetus happens when past associations and affinities block the soul's path. Ancient debts and ancestral issues need clarification before you can pursue the path of your destiny. What you experience as personal melancholy may be a collective ancestral suffering that needs attention.

UPRIGHT You are suddenly let down, and regret places you temporarily in the past. Friendships, partnerships and relationships have a shaky basis or are without real love. Plans cannot be completed, but consider what options remain.

REVERSED Hope returns after a loss and promises expectations that are more pleasant. Reunions herald the strengthening of old affinities or the healing of rifts that have divided you. You find a new cause to support.

DISCONNECTED Your fear of a secret flaw, an ancestral or genetic inheritance, leaves you stranded between isolation and association with those whom you love. Or perhaps you are the lone survivor of a lost cause? Reappraise the fears or affinities that still overshadow you, and seek clarity.

SIX *of* WATER

MEMORY

DIMMI

How does the past pave the way to the future?

STUDY OF A UNICORN LOWERING ITS

HORN TO DRINK

BACKGROUND Leonardo counsels the artist to carry a notebook, taking care not to rub out sketches, 'for the infinite forms and dispositions of objects are such that memory cannot retain them without these guides and mentors'.

SOUL-CODE The signposts of memory enable the soul to recall the experiences of past existences. With this knowledge, the route by which you arrived at this moment is neither shameful nor troubling, but can guide you on the destined path to the fulfilment of your soul's gift.

UPRIGHT Memory strengthens connection with things that were before. Childhood places, old loves, past associations call to you. Longing acts as a spur either to encourage growth or to remain stuck in the past.

REVERSED The past falls behind and is regenerated as the future. Opportunities are stirring, heralding new vistas. Old ways of doing and behaving can be replaced by new ways that your experience shows you.

DISCONNECTED There is a compulsive need to return to past events, to revisit the shame, regret or degradation. You are sunk in the past, clinging to the wreckage of what once floated. Reassess, and live in the present moment.

SEVEN *of* WATER

ILLUSION

SEVEN *of* WATER
ILLUSION

DIMMI

What story have you spun around this matter?

STUDY FOR A DOG WHICH BECOMES A BAT
WHEN INVERTED

BACKGROUND Leonardo writes, 'Have we not seen pictures so closely resembling the real thing that their illusion tricks both man and beast?' He considered the artist's ability to deceive the viewer a divine skill, though one which artists must use with integrity.

SOUL-CODE Discrimination brings the clear light by which the soul steers on the road to its destiny. It is essential to be able to discern between reality and the mirage, so that you are not led from your road. What glitters is not always gold, nor can you midwife all your dreams from sleeping into waking. Whatever the imagination shapes grows more real the longer you consider it.

UPRIGHT Illusions and wish-fulfilment are clouding your vision. Learn to discriminate between reality and fantasy. Daydreams only manifest if there is substance and energy behind them. Creatively pursue your dreams, but ground them in everyday life before you rely on them.

REVERSED Clear, resolute vision will help you achieve your desires, and intelligent choices will help you decide and determine. Clear away the fog of illusion.

DISCONNECTED People do not share your vision. Self-delusion and foolish desires have led you into dangerous areas. Come into focus.

EIGHT *of* WATER

TRANSPORT

DIMMI
How can your plan be improved?

PLAN FOR AN AUTOMOBILE

BACKGROUND Leonardo's theoretical understanding of the combustion engine didn't reveal to him how it might be applied to this first blueprint of an automobile. But then, 'Men might stay peacefully in bed if their imaginations were satisfied.'

SOUL-CODE Adjustment and reorientation helps the soul remain true to its destiny. What you have planned doesn't always work out, and it would be but wasted effort to continue knowing that your dream will crash. As your soul matures, so early wishes and hopes lose their attraction. You are led to seek and explore more deeply.

UPRIGHT Mature reassessment leads you to consider the abandonment of old plans. Something is not working out satisfactorily, and will merely waste your time and resources unless you discontinue. Go deeper, seek further.

REVERSED Something you began a long time ago is now coming into its own. Old debts and commitments you felt had been broken have been repaid or restitution made to you. You are reinstated and accepted. Have a party!

DISCONNECTED An aimless search for happiness unsettles you. Alienation or abandonment keeps you in a state of emotional discontent. Escaping from intimacy or commitment makes you a pilgrim who doesn't want to arrive at the shrine.

NINE *of* WATER

AIRBORNE

NINE *of* WATER
AIRBORNE

DIMMI
What is your heart's desire?

A MAN IN FLIGHT

BACKGROUND Leonardo's greatest wish was to be airborne. 'A man complete with sufficiently large wings might learn to overcome air-resistance and conquer the air by raising himself upon it.' His secret plan to fly from Mount Ceceri may never have happened.

SOUL-CODE Fulfilment of the heart's wish brings satisfaction to the soul. This attainment of desire enables you to enjoy the unfolding path of your destiny with pleasure and ease. Remember that material success is merely incidental and not the reward for the soul's labours, for these cannot be measured by gain.

UPRIGHT Wishes, plans and associations can be successfully achieved. You can enjoy a sense of well-being, abundance and pleasure. Beware of self-indulgence or becoming complacent, when the time for enjoyment has passed.

REVERSED Concealed mistakes surface and change everything. A massive flaw underlies your plans, wishes and relationships. Past achievements are no guide to results. Check the tides and currents before proceeding.

DISCONNECTED Just because your wishes crash-landed doesn't mean they won't fly another day. A misspent youth or a tendency towards self-indulgence can keep you solitary, even among your friends. Simplicity of life will help you.

TEN *of* WATER

FAMILY

DIMMI
What is returning home?

SKETCH OF THE HOLY FAMILY

TEN *of* WATER
FAMILY

BACKGROUND In this study for the Virgin and St Anne, Christ leans down delightedly to touch a lamb, affirming his own destiny as the Lamb of God and the incarnate Saviour who makes everyone kin with him.

SOUL-CODE The emotional satisfaction of homecoming reflects the soul's deepest wish for union and the end of travelling. Although the path of destiny is still to be fully explored, it is good to rest and be appreciated in the bosom of your family or the heart of your community. There is honour for the seeker who comes home to the place where his heart is.

UPRIGHT The security of home and native land gives you peace and contentment. Environmental harmony or a secure reputation brings happiness. A guest is welcomed home, and there is a civic reception or receipt of honours.

REVERSED Homecoming is delayed, or the plan is coming unstuck. Disruptions and incompatibilities are signs of the opposition to you settling down. Community or tribe outlaw you, and you experience impatience with family members.

DISCONNECTED You want to return home and demonstrate how well you've done, but there is little to show and so you stay away. Don't let the opinions and pettiness of others keep you nomadic or a scapegoat forever.

PAGE *of* WATER

PAGE *of* WATER

DIMMI

What needs your support?

SALAI

BACKGROUND Gian Giacomo Caprotti, nicknamed Salai (Little Devil), entered Leonardo's service in 1490 as a model and general assistant. Salai was a roguish urchin who initially stole from his master but later became his trusted agent.

SOUL-CODE Devotion to the soul's path brings you safely to the heart of your destiny. The ability to bring harmony and good feeling to those around you arouses tenderness in the hearts of others. As a servant of love, your task is to awaken desire and attraction, opening imaginative pathways that will be fruitful.

UPRIGHT You are devoted, trustworthy and likeable, willing to be of service. Apply yourself to research or study with loving enthusiasm. It is appropriate to support someone or be a confidant. Keep a light, playful attitude if you are starting a relationship.

REVERSED Disinclined and a little too charming, you are aesthetically hung up on the inessentials. Fashion-conscious or susceptible to peer pressure, you follow the pack rather than individual taste. Your veneer of romanticism is a cover for self-interest.

DISCONNECTED Vulnerability makes you resistant and afraid of love. Unrealistic expectations or a certain naivety keeps you locked in a dream. Fantasies, romantic scenarios or imaginary friends mean more to you than the life around you.

KNIGHT *of* WATER

KNIGHT *of* WATER

DIMMI

How do you feel about this?

SKETCH FOR A FESTIVAL COSTUME

BACKGROUND This elaborately costumed knight was created by Leonardo for the Duke of Milan's masque. It is clear, from his beribboned and unarmoured state, that he rides in the lists of love rather than in the theatre of war.

SOUL-CODE Emotional satisfaction is an essential food for the soul. By diving deeply into the waters of the psyche, you discover fundamental clues to the art of soul-making. Destiny's path unfolds when the gifts of a responsive heart are realized. As a guardian of love, you invite the awakened desire to deeper intimacy and fulfilment.

UPRIGHT Your emotional appeal opens all the doors, making you attractive. Ideals and visions bloom. Kindness and a patient gentleness can help friends or lovers to become receptive or intimate. Proposals and invitations come your way.

REVERSED You are plying your art to deceive and benefit. Emotional dishonesty or sexual manipulation motivate your schemes. You play the field as a seducer by sleeping around, or indulge in narcissistic self-regard.

DISCONNECTED You are submerged in a miasmic or misty romanticism. Idealistic dreams of 'true love' are the barrier keeping you from making lasting attachments. Dispel the illusions of love and welcome its reality.

LADY *of* WATER

LADY *of* WATER

DIMMI

What does your compassion tell you?

STUDY OF THE HEAD OF A YOUNG WOMAN

BACKGROUND This reflective study, with its submissive bowed neck, gives us some idea that it was intended by Leonardo to portray a Madonna leaning over her child.

SOUL-CODE Sensitivity is the courtesy of the soul, enabling you to feel your way towards your destiny. The ability to sense undercurrents and subtle nuances keeps you from emotional misunderstandings. Psychic or intuitional messages must be scanned for content and reality, or they may lead you astray. When you exercise compassion you become a loving mother to those about you.

UPRIGHT Beloved because of your emotional capacity and sensitivity, your compassion makes you an intimate confidant. A love of beauty creates harmonious surroundings. Visionary and compassionate approaches must be taken. Someone needs comfort or advice.

REVERSED Your emotional immaturity and inconsistency sends the wrong signals. Take care not to use emotional blackmail. You are susceptible to mystic flights of fancy, or become englamoured too easily. Beware the grip of addictions.

DISCONNECTED Hypersensitivity or psychic resistance stampedes you into hostility and suspicion. An unworldliness surrounds you, making you prey to people's projections. Spend more time in the world of the everyday.

LORD *of* WATER

LORD *of* WATER

DIMMI

Where is the emotional satisfaction?

STUDY OF A BEARDED MAN

BACKGROUND This portrait of a bearded man was made in 1513, when Leonardo took his entourage to Rome to enter the service of the rather dreamy courtier Giuliano de' Medici, of whom this may be a romantic likeness.

SOUL-CODE Unconditional love and support are the gifts that encourage the soul to develop without fear. A generous outlook widens the path to destiny and leaves gratitude in the wake of a life well lived. Beware of becoming self-regarding in your charity, for he who loves without thought of reward does not need any accolade. When you consider others, you become a loving father and benefactor to those around you.

UPRIGHT You are considerate and wise, honourable and fair, and your liberal views make you an advocate of sympathetic integrity. Creatively sensitive to events, you bring peace and harmony. Congenial and artistic pursuits flourish.

REVERSED Dishonourable and swift to take advantage, or heartless and crafty, you explore the potential of exploitation. Sentimental or wimpish behaviour covers self-interest. You are emotionally unavailable or evasive. Commitments are betrayed.

DISCONNECTED Indulgence in self-inverted fantasies helps you fake it. Maintain your practice, not a facade. Dependencies shore you up, and over-protective attitudes smother growth. The world won't exploit you if you risk showing love.

ACE *of* EARTH

EARTH

DIMMI
What is of value?

STUDY OF A LANDSCAPE

ACE *of* EARTH
EARTH

BACKGROUND Leonardo was one of the first Italian painters to attend closely to landscape. 'Go to the countryside over valleys and mountains ... which you can only enjoy with your own eyes ... rather than listening to a poet's description.'

SOUL-CODE Good fortune is a magnet which attracts prosperity. Possession is an opportunity for the soul to learn about responsibility and living lightly upon the earth. The path of destiny unfolds felicitously when material accomplishments are fused with a practical spiritual wisdom. The path of earth ensures you grapple with the *prima materia* of life, like an alchemist who starts with first principles and eventually achieves gold.

UPRIGHT Practical wisdom, good fortune and prosperity are yours. A new vista brings happiness and well-being. Use this opportunity to seek intrinsic worth and value. A gift is given, and you enjoy material accomplishment and satisfaction.

REVERSED You experience a run of good fortune, but wealth and gain don't always bring the joy you hoped – just more responsibility. Material goods can't substitute true worth. Beware that the glitter of gold doesn't make you greedy or miserly.

DISCONNECTED Don't hold back because something looks too good to be true. Reassess how and why you value things, without sentimentality. Your soul cannot be bought and sold.

TWO *of* EARTH

POLARITY

DIMMI
What makes you feel ambivalent?

DIAGRAM OF A CRANK

BACKGROUND This crank creates a back-and-forth motion by means of a rod and wheel which moves either end of the shaft. 'Nothing capable of movement is more powerful ... than its mover.'

SOUL-CODE The principles of polarity enable the soul to distinguish the balance of two extremes. Darkness and light, up and down, in and out, are rhythms that follow each other in succession. The path of destiny is subject to the rules of polarity which, like light and shadow, cause things to look good or bad as you travel through life. Finding the point of balance will help you journey on without undue elation or depression.

UPRIGHT Choice brings ambivalence. You have difficulty in getting started or adapting to changing situations. Multiplicity or bureaucratic entanglements confuse things as you try to launch yourself. Your fortunes swing like a pendulum.

REVERSED Look at both sides of the market to assess where you stand. Holding two ideas in one place is no difficulty for you, since you handle complexity well. Double-accounting can sabotage you.

DISCONNECTED Complexity is becoming your master. Trying to keep all sides covered means that you serve none. Stand back and assess what can be delegated or discarded. Step off the treadmill.

THREE *of* EARTH

PERSPECTIVE

DIMMI

What viewpoint is guiding or confusing the issue?

THREE *of* EARTH
PERSPECTIVE

AN ARTIST WITH PERSPECTIVE
VIEWFINDER AND GLOBE

BACKGROUND Artists learned the nature of perspective through this 'perspectograph'. Leonardo wrote that 'Perspective is the bridle and rudder of painting ... nothing less than a thorough knowledge of the function of the eye.'

SOUL-CODE The soul needs a sense of perspective to help refine the map of destiny. By evaluating the sightings in any given situation, the soul gains dignity and perfection. Your ability to master the appointed task and to apply yourself to fulfilling the promise of your destiny gives you renown and respect. Perspective is your guide and teacher.

UPRIGHT A sense of perspective gives you skill and artistry. Your well-earned reputation precedes you, and opens the way to further commissions. Patronage and support back up what you have planned.

REVERSED Mediocrity is the enemy. What you are producing is too commonplace and doesn't do justice to the originality of your plans. Sloppy work or being wasteful of resources diminishes your efforts and your reputation.

DISCONNECTED You feel out of focus or unable to bring improvement from your standpoint. Get another opinion, another point of view. You are neither incapable nor inefficient. Old voices that say you are must be evicted.

FOUR *of* EARTH

ASSEMBLY

DIMMI
Who is controlling what?

FOUR *of* EARTH
ASSEMBLY

SKETCH FOR THE LAST SUPPER

BACKGROUND The Last Supper explores the potential for the disciples to share friendship amidst the plotting of Judas – the purse-holder of the Twelve – to betray their leader for the sake of financial reward.

SOUL-CODE The control of resources is a responsible task. Whoever apportions the goods must share out fairly. It is a mistake for the soul to become too attached to the means by which power, money and position are gained. Instead of furthering the flow of life, your destiny becomes interwoven with the control of territory and the manipulation of others for gain.

UPRIGHT You assert your territory or call the shots. Generosity controls your turf. Establishment is won by bribes and handouts, and your love of money and power masks meanness or hoarding. Learn to share without strings.

REVERSED Let go of your control. There are obstacles to you gaining more. Delays and blocks encourage you to speculate, risk or be spendthrift. Prestige and power are hard-won. Learn to live more simply.

DISCONNECTED Defensiveness armours you. You cling to connections or possessions that have depreciated, and look to others to protect you – but at a price. Someone controls your actions.

FIVE *of* EARTH

NEED

FIVE *of* EARTH
NEED

DIMMI
How is need shaping your destiny?

ENVY RIDES ON A SKELETON

BACKGROUND Fear of poverty drives everyone: 'A malignant thing of great terror will so far spread among men that, in their panic to avoid it, they will only succeed in increasing its limitless powers.' This image shows how desire and need are connected.

SOUL-CODE Need is the common ground for the soul's training, providing realistic lessons about manifesting your destiny. From the perspective of need you see all things with insight, from the high-flown plans that never fully emerge to the basic necessities without which life is so difficult. Need helps you focus and value what you have, and be less profligate and more appreciative of your resources.

UPRIGHT Trouble, loss and instability make you feel impoverished and needy. Resources are scanty – supply doesn't meet demand. Material obstacles create difficulty. Reappreciate your innate gift in both sickness and health.

REVERSED There is a way through the present time, and the tide of bad luck is beginning to ebb. Imaginative solutions can be found if you dig deep into your resourcefulness.

DISCONNECTED Profligacy with your resources may have led to misfortune, or it may be that separation has been a necessary part of survival. Return from exile to begin again.

SIX *of* EARTH

GIVING

DIMMI

What can you give?

A STUDY OF THE VIRGIN'S HAND

BACKGROUND Leonardo writes: 'The actions of hands and arms must be connected to the intention of the mind that moves them. Whoever has a sympathetic understanding will follow the lead of his intentions in all the motions of his hands.' Unmotivated gestures look empty and meaningless, but, through the fusion of the body with the mind, gestures become significant.

SOUL-CODE Generosity arises from a heart in tune with circumstances. The ability to give without expectation arises in those who are secure in their destiny. The treasury of your soul cannot be spent or given away to vain ends. It is currency that will provide you with resources and the ability to handle responsibilities without betrayal or greed.

UPRIGHT Generosity, gifts, support, kindness or benefactors make things feel secure. Spontaneous giving and help comes unexpectedly. Kindness and reciprocation aid true exchange.

REVERSED Resources are shorter than you imagined. The payout on your investment is lower than you expected. You may have taken generosity for granted. Beware that envy doesn't make you opportunist.

DISCONNECTED Denying your own needs is foolish. If you don't ask, you won't get. It is time to ask for the help that you need.

SEVEN *of* EARTH

STAMINA

DIMMI
Where must you invest stamina?

SKETCH OF A HORSE

SEVEN *of* EARTH
STAMINA

BACKGROUND This horse is another sketch for the Sforza monument that Leonardo laboured over. 'The energy in every living creature comes from the vital spark of the soul, and all vital power descends from the sun itself.'

SOUL-CODE Stamina keeps the soul pursuing the path of destiny with a good will. You neither halt upon the way nor rest upon your laurels in finding ways to manifest your destiny. Stamina is maintained by finding a natural rhythm of work and rest, rather than by ceaseless activity and snatched repose. Appraise your work from time to time, to ensure consistent quality.

UPRIGHT Ingenuity and hard work have led to growth. Continual achievement is maintained by continual effort; exertion, stamina, patience are still needed. Pace yourself if the task in hand is long or unwieldy.

REVERSED Worries about loss or suspicions of resources diminishing or being stolen allow you little rest. Keep a close eye on things, especially if others are supposed to be vigilant for you. Check that investments are prospering.

DISCONNECTED Owning the work of your hands and taking credit for it may be difficult, but keep going. Fear of success may sabotage you. Make good decisions about where and with whom you work.

EIGHT *of* EARTH

LABOUR

DIMMI
Where are your skills needed?

SKETCHES OF MEN WORKING

EIGHT *of* EARTH
LABOUR

BACKGROUND Leonardo explored the versatility of the human form by watching men at work: 'I shall represent Labour by showing pulling, thrusting, carrying, stopping, supporting and other actions,' he writes.

SOUL-CODE By keeping up your spiritual practice, your soul labours to create the Great Work, which is nothing less than the bringing together of microcosm and macrocosm. When this is achieved, the path of destiny becomes manifest upon Earth as well as in Heaven. Having pride in your craft means choosing the best materials and tools, and maintaining the skills to use them.

UPRIGHT Perfecting your craft in a dedicated way hones your efficiency. The effort of continual practice is worthwhile. Deal with things purposefully and without guile; your word and your work are your promise.

REVERSED Your work is getting lost in the detail, or workaholism is taking its toll. Lack of ambition feeds idleness and lack of engagement. You cut corners, leaving work to others, or living off their resources and skills.

DISCONNECTED Lack of skills or focus keeps you idle. Disillusionment with work traps you in dead-end jobs. Return to the thing you most wanted to do, and reassess how you could retrain.

NINE *of* EARTH

ROOTS

NINE *of* EARTH
ROOTS

DIMMI

Where is your rightful place? What is the necessary attitude to take here?

TREES DIP THEIR ROOTS INTO A STREAM

BACKGROUND In his *Treatise on Painting*, Leonardo wrote: 'the tree-rings transecting a branch determine the tree's age, while the larger and smaller rings show the wet or dry years of its growth.' The exposed roots of these trees reveal whence the tree takes its strength.

SOUL-CODE Maturity of soul is gained only when life experience has sunk deep roots strong enough to support you. These roots enable you to walk the path of destiny with confident connection, and to stand tall in your rightful place. Stability helps you cultivate your interests more deeply.

UPRIGHT You reach a place of accomplishment through discretion, prudence and forethought, and enjoy contentment and a sense of expansion after struggling for so long. This is an affluent time, or a time for pursuing hobbies.

REVERSED Security and luxury can be honeyed traps into which you sink with false expectation. Ensure that you have covered your back against threats, thefts, extortions or deceits of others.

DISCONNECTED You have been struggling on, when you could have stopped. You rounded the hill some time back: stop climbing and looking back down. Enjoy the view and rejoice.

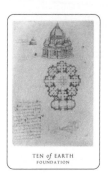

TEN *of* EARTH

FOUNDATION

DIMMI

What have you inherited? How are you enriched?

GROUND-PLAN AND ELEVATION OF A BASILICA

BACKGROUND This plan is based upon Classical centrality rather than the medieval nave cathedral. Leonardo notes that 'For stability, the depths of the foundations in ... temples and other public buildings should be in proportion to the weight that will rest upon them.'

SOUL-CODE The soul must be grafted onto solid foundations and sustained by beneficial nurture. These foundations are provided by the riches of the generational family stock, which becomes the inheritance and background for the soul to live out its destiny. A stable environment brings security and growth of wisdom.

UPRIGHT The security of home and family encloses you. Draw upon the genetic or financial inheritance from your ancestry to enrich and guide you. Received wisdom and ancestral sagacity protect the future.

REVERSED Turning your back on traditions and family, you reject your inheritance in order to make your own way. You must endure the hazards this brings, and you risk uncertainty if you choose this path.

DISCONNECTED Your heritage is charged with conflicting issues that you also inherit. This makes the world seem unsafe, shadowing work, relationships and pathways that you fail to take because of old associations. Ancestral healing is needed.

PAGE *of* EARTH

PAGE *of* EARTH

DIMMI

How is this useful?

STUDY OF ST PHILIP FOR THE LAST SUPPER

BACKGROUND At Christ's feeding of the five thousand, the apostle Philip enquired how they might all be fed. Here he gazes with trustful longing at his Master, wondering how anyone could betray him.

SOUL-CODE Application and patient tenacity help bring the soul steadily along the path of destiny. You follow the signs and move ahead, learning as you proceed. You collect information and shift its usefulness, but you also share it with others. When you recognize the true value of others, you are a loyal servant of wisdom.

UPRIGHT A hard worker, you are pragmatic, realistic and loyal. Work proceeds steadily by daily application. This is a good time to research, learn a new skill or be deeply studious. A message about contracts or business matters is likely to be received.

REVERSED Practical matters fall through your grasp. The obvious is not obvious to you; rebellion and reaction shape what you see. You may be handling too many things. Beware of giving up study or falling into inertia.

DISCONNECTED You have lost focus and attention. By listening to the cellular information stored in your body, you will find wisdom and become properly grounded. Attend to the real issue of how you live effectively.

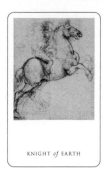

KNIGHT *of* EARTH

KNIGHT *of* EARTH

DIMMI

What needs to be properly grounded?

SKETCH OF A RIDER ON A REARING HORSE

BACKGROUND Leonardo writes, 'Man and animals suffer greater fatigue in going uphill than going downhill. On the ascent he carries his weight with him, on the descent he merely lets go.'

SOUL-CODE Reliability and patience enable the soul to pursue the path of destiny. Attention to detail helps to formulate consistent results and the creation of a method that can be relied upon. Service is your duty. When you respond to those who depend upon you, you are a practical guardian of wisdom who makes things safe.

UPRIGHT You are orderly, reliable and persistent in your efforts. Your realistic and practical eye assesses risk with good judgement. Dependable in all things, people rely on you. Trust and security come from your protection.

REVERSED You can be inert and unresponsive, determined to have a quiet life. A deeply materialistic viewpoint can make you morose or unimaginative. Neglectful and self-centred, you can be a stick-in-the-mud or a deserter.

DISCONNECTED Fears of abandonment and neglect keep you out of the circle. Better to be lost than abandoned again, you think, but unless you engage yourself you won't realize how much you are appreciated.

LADY *of* EARTH

LADY *of* EARTH

DIMMI

What is enough or not enough?

STUDY FOR AN ANGEL

BACKGROUND This study of a young girl made in 1483 was the model of the angel that appears in Leonardo's painting the *Madonna of the Rocks*, where he made the figure asexual in accordance with the angelic subject.

SOUL-CODE A sense of prosperity comes from abundance of soul rather than from wealth. You have the ability to make things comfortable and secure wherever you go, using few resources and whatever the circumstances. The path of destiny for you is not about your own comfort alone. When you share your resources generously, you are a wise mother to those about you.

UPRIGHT You take a wholistic approach to life, sharing your hospitality and love of comfort with those who need stability. Your support is one hundred per cent. Things run smoothly, and prosperity and resourcefulness prevail.

REVERSED Possessiveness is a sign that you suspect and distrust those nearest to you. You are disorganized or over-organized, and are not comfortable in yourself. Hoarding or squandering resources clutters or depletes your life.

DISCONNECTED You fear scarcity or feel inadequate to perform. A dread of insecurity warps your enjoyment of life. A sense of helplessness can be overcome when you see how your achievements can support you.

LORD *of* EARTH

DIMMI

How can you bring stability?

PORTRAIT OF A MAN

BACKGROUND This impressive drawing may be of Gian Giacomo Trivulzio, the *condottiere* and former enemy of Ludovico Sforza. Leonardo was engaged to create a monumental tomb for him.

SOUL-CODE Guardianship of the land and your community is a responsibility that brings stability to the soul. When the common good is safeguarded, you can pursue the path of destiny in the knowledge that you have contributed and done your duty. You have provided and given wise guidance. When you protect your family or provide security for dependants, you are a wise father.

UPRIGHT Leadership and business acumen make you beneficent and prosperous. Endurance and pragmatism give you strong foundations. A deep love of the land and an upholding of traditional values creates both quality of life and stability.

REVERSED You can be manipulative and corrupt in your dealings. Acquisitive and financially exploitative, your materialism overturns respect for land and people. Miserliness and a narrow possessive outlook constrain things.

DISCONNECTED A deep insecurity about being undervalued and constantly put down by an authority figure keeps you small and contracted. Begin to encourage yourself step by step, and strip away your old destabilizing attitude.

5

THE SEAT OF THE SOUL

SPREADS AND READINGS

'The faculty of judgement that is given to man is quickened by the way that the five senses are conjoined in the perceptive organ known as the "sensus communis" . . . which is the seat of the soul. . . . The sense waits upon the soul, and not the soul on the sense, for it is a minister of the soul.'

— LEONARDO DA VINCI

GETTING STARTED

Although you can use *The Da Vinci Enigma Tarot* to lay any of the tarot spreads with which you may already be familiar, there are a number of new spreads offered here that will help you explore the pack's unique wisdom. The first three spreads – Vitruvian Man, Cause and Effect, and The Divine Proportion – all follow the standard convention of laying each card on a given position. The Destiny spread, however, requires a greater degree of skill and flexibility, as you will discover, so don't try this one until you feel ready.

If you are new to tarot, it is a good idea to get a sense of how the cards interact with you and your questions by drawing just a few cards to begin with. Try a few of the following basic card-reading patterns to get started, encouraged by Leonardo's advice. Compose a concise question to ask the cards.

LIGHT AND SHADOW 'Light chases away darkness. Shadow obstructs light.' Cut the pack into two piles, turning over the topmost card of each pile. The first represents the light shining on your issue, the second is the shadow or unknown factors that it carries. Consider your question in relationship to the meanings. Answer the dimmi question for each card.

THE CHERRY TREE 'The tips of the topmost cherry-tree branches form a pyramid at their crown.' Cut the pack into three piles and turn over the topmost three cards, placing them in a triangle. The card at the apex represents what you aim for, the left-hand card is what hinders it, and the right-hand card is what helps it.

THE PAINTER'S FOUR SEASONS 'He is a poor student who doesn't excel his master.' Shuffle or mix the cards, drawing four. The first is *Beginner*, or the basis of the question, the second *Apprentice*, or what you have to learn about it, the third *Journeyman*, or what action you must take about it, and the fourth *Master*, or what inspires you about it.

THE SOURCE 'Go to the school of nature rather than to copies of nature; go to the fountain, not to the water jar.' Starting from the top of the pack, keep turning over cards until you come to a macrocosm card. Take this card as your *Source* and the three cards directly underneath it as your *Water jars*. The Source is the water that nourishes you, card 2 shows what is stale and needs to be tipped away, card 3 shows what needs to be mixed in, and card 4 is where your water is flowing.

SOUL'S INTENTIONS 'The two main goals of the painter are to depict man and his soul's intention.' Again, starting from the top of the pack, keep turning over the cards until you come to a court card – your central card. This is an aspect of yourself, and the four cards directly following it show: what face you show to the world; what you hide from the world; the face of which you are ashamed; and the face you have yet to develop. Starting at the top and moving clockwise, place these four cards around the middle court card, reading all four in relation to it.

VITRUVIAN MAN SPREAD

Vitruvian Man shows the perfect human being who has discovered the point of integration between the macrocosm and the microcosm. This harmonious balance allows him to walk both in the everyday world but also in the Otherworld, and see issues with an integrated perspective. We may notice that the man in this image looks like a self-portrait of Leonardo himself. This spread gives a general overview and a good perspective of the issue.

Compose your question, shuffle the cards, and lay them upon positions 1–10, without reference to the design on the backs of the cards (change the numeration for the dominant-/supporting-hand positions according to whether you are left- or right-handed; the illustration shows the positions for a right-handed person). The meanings of the card positions are as follows:

1 HEART What your feelings and instincts experience about the issue.

2 DOMINANT HAND How you conventionally deal with this issue.

3 SUPPORTING HAND What instinctive skills and gifts you can draw upon to help transform this.

4 RIGHT FOOT How you have paved the way for this to come about.

5 LEFT FOOT How you can prevent walking into such issues in future.

6 WHAT IS WITHIN YOUR GRASP What you can achieve, if you reach for it.

7 WHAT NEEDS TO CHANGE What you need to change, give away or remove to attain your goal.

8 WHERE YOUR STEPS ARE LED Reveals the opportunities that will guide you now.

9 HOW TO TAKE THE NEXT STEP How you can use the gift of this present moment to step forward.

10 HEAD Shows you the wisdom of fresh motivation.

Consult either the upright or reversed meanings, according to how your cards are laid down. If you have questions or difficulties relating to any of the cards, refer to the 'disconnected' meaning of that specific card to help integrate understanding.

SAMPLE READING

Diane is an artist whose work is being sold via a small gallery. She is dissatisfied with the way the gallery owner deals with her but, since it is her first major exhibition, feels reluctant to say anything. She is already aware that her inability to market and promote herself is causing problems, so she asks: *'How can I speak up for myself in this situation?'*

After shuffling in her question, she checks the Guide Cards, which show *Page of Earth, Four of Water/Disappointment,* and *Lord of Water.* Just looking at the pictures on these cards gives her an immediate feeling of 'yes – this is me and my situation'. The innocent page, the disappointment in an enterprise, and the handsome but unapproachable man who stands for the gallery owner underlie the reading. Reassembling the deck, she lays the following cards:

1 *Three of Water/Conjunction* Deep down, Diane feels that there can be a rapprochement with the gallery owner, for although she is only one lone artist her art contributes to the profits that keep his gallery running.

2 *XI Experience* If left to her own devices, she would perhaps sit on her feelings of unfairness and say nothing, just feeling more and more hard-done-by, but the card of Experience says to honour her own integrity.

3 *IX Hermit* The Hermit urges her to seek her own deep counsels in the silence of her heart, to weigh up what is really going on here.

4 *Two of Earth/Polarity* (reversed) This card shows that her innate sense of fairness may lead her into situations where she ignores both sides of a contract. She automatically trusts people of status and authority in ways that lead her into trouble.

5 *XVIII Conception* By looking out for duplicity, perhaps even expecting that not everyone is going to treat her with respect, Diane can prevent herself getting trapped again in a disadvantageous situation.

6 *XVII Way-Shower* (reversed) Diane needs to understand that physical attraction is no guide to someone's motivations and intentions. By following charismatic people, she denies her own inner guidance.

7 *Eight of Earth/Labour* Owning her own work and taking the credit for it is a big part of what needs to change. Although she will always value the opinion of others, and indeed depend on the appreciation of her public, if she doesn't take care of her work someone else will profit more than she does.

8 *XV Pain & Pleasure* The opportunity is now upon her to face up to the fear of what binds her in this pattern. Her attraction/repulsion for the gallery owner must shift into a more neutral artist–agent relationship, or she will remain endlessly fascinated by such powerful but abusive people.

9 *Ace of Fire* This card gives Diane the go-ahead to implement this advice. By contemplating the creative impetus of her work, she can face up to the gallery owner: even if she fails, she will gain self-respect and feel that she has defended both her art and herself.

10 *VIII Strength* Her fresh motivation is strength and the need to defend her self-respect. Her passion for life will bring her through this encounter.

OVERVIEW In this ten-card reading, six cards are macrocosm cards, showing that Diane is grappling with some of the most fundamentally important issues that will shape her life. Her soul's destiny as an artist is worth defending. There is one Water card, one Fire card and two Earth cards, but no Air cards, indicating that it is time she applied her intelligence to this situation, and stopped placing the responsibility for decision-making in the hands of others.

CAUSE AND EFFECT SPREAD

Leonardo's observation of the fundamental principles of cause and effect inspires this spread. He writes, 'What marvellous, extraordinary necessity! who by supreme reason compels all effects to be the direct result of their causes. By its supreme and irrevocable law, every natural action obeys neces- sity by the shortest possible process.'

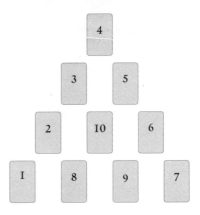

Use this spread to take a closer look at how you are involved in the causation of things in your life; you will be guided to a deeper understand- ing and increased vigilance in all your actions, thoughts and plans. Compose your question, shuffle the cards, and lay them in positions 1–10 as shown. The meanings are as follows:

1 Ancestors/Origins/Roots: this is where the issue is rooted in the past.
2 What you bring from the past about this issue.
3 The cause or trigger of the issue in the present time.
4 The issue itself.
5 The effect of the issue upon everything around you.
6 What you take to the future about this issue.
7 Descendants/Fruit/Outcome: how the issue affects the future.
8 Hopes. Your positive attitude. Self-help.
9 Fears. Your negative attitude. Self-sabotage.
10 The truth about the issue: this gives you the core intention to change.

As you read the cards, note the connections between cards 3 and 8, 5 and 9, 4 and 10, and 1 and 7.

SAMPLE READING

Gerald was about to undergo surgery and was understandably anxious. He asked: 'Show me what I need to know about my operation and its aftermath.' He didn't bother with Guide Cards.

1 *Ten of Water/Family* This revealed that the root cause of Gerald's illness arose from his attempt to keep his family together in a safe environment for many years. Gerald

had worked over-hard to provide security.

2 *XVI Deluge* Gerald brought with him a sense of humiliation and loss of pride in being no longer able to be the breadwinner. If the surgery were successful, however, he would be able to work again. At the moment, he was too stunned to consider this.

3 *Page of Water* (reversed) This showed that Gerald was afraid of submerging himself into the unknown. A stubborn pride had kept him from listening to good advice that might have prevented the escalation of his illness.

4 *XII Passover* Held in a kind of suspended animation, Gerald had come to a point of no return. The Passover card revealed the heart of the issue. Something had to be sacrificed or he would remain eternally stuck, neither living nor dying. The operation itself was a massive hurdle for him, and had already been postponed more than once.

5 *Page of Air* This card showed Gerald looking at the crisis and troubleshooting it to the best of his ability. His defensiveness and avoidance of the situation clearly would not serve him now. In future, he might be much more vigilant and procrastinate less, which would clarify matters for everyone. This card also felt connected with the surgeon, whose clear-sighted skill would resolve things.

6 *Three of Earth/Perspective* This revealed that Gerald would take a better sense of perspective into the future, and be able to make improvements. As this was a card of the craftsman, it felt as if he would be able to re-engage his skills and work again.

7 *Two of Earth/Polarity* The effect upon everyone around him might be to make them more aware of the need to balance up the family relationship, and be less dependent upon him.

8 *Lady of Water* This revealed Gerald's hopes. His longing for emotional reciprocation and comfort was foremost at this time. He admitted to watching old sentimental black-and-white films to help boost his confidence.

9 *IX Hermit* For Gerald, the worst thought was the fear of being left alone. His ability to be solitary or introspective was very limited.

10 *II Enigma* With an unknown outcome to his surgery, Gerald was doubtful about such a mystical card in this position. I pointed out that this card was the midwife of the issue at position 4, where he was currently stuck. This surgery was an opportunity

to break through to a deeper Gerald who could achieve his inner dreams and appreciate the wisdom that he had gained during his life.

OVERVIEW Cards 1 and 7 hinted at relationship issues with his family. Cards 2 and 6 showed a progression from being shocked and muddled to a much greater clarity and control. Cards 3 and 5 revealed an emotional immaturity that had led to the issue at card 4. Cards 8 and 3 showed an old romantic who just wanted to be loved. Cards 9 and 5 spoke of a fearful man who was being led to a much more mature outlook on life. The illness and the operation were part of a much bigger development in his life, as could be seen by pairing cards 4 and 10. The surgery was successful to such an extent that Gerald's whole outlook on life has changed.

THE DIVINE PROPORTION SPREAD

Leonardo was a student of the mathematician Luca Pacioli, whose book *The Divine Proportion* strove to prove that the Golden Ratio was a symbol of the Creator and divine harmony. The Golden Ratio was first propounded by Euclid of Alexandria in 300 BCE, and is an expression of Phi, or 1.618033988749895. Euclid drew a line so that the ratio of the entire line, A, to the length of line B, is the same as the ratio of B to the length of the smaller line, C. A is thus 1.618… times B, and B is 1.618… times C.

$$A \qquad\qquad\qquad\qquad B \qquad\qquad\qquad\qquad C$$

We may see the long line A as the macrocosm, and the smaller line B as the microcosm. The complex simplicity of the Golden Ratio is displayed everywhere in nature: in the spiral curve of a nautilus shell; in the growth patterns of plants; in the structure of DNA; and in buildings like the Parthenon, as well as in the solar system itself. Leonardo made continual use of this proportion in his paintings, noting it in nature in the growth of trees. This diagram (*right*) shows a series of nested Golden Rectangles. This sequence of diminishing rectangles is based upon the line of the Golden Ratio, creating what has been called 'the eye of God', and forms the basis for this spread. The Divine Proportion Spread draws upon the Golden

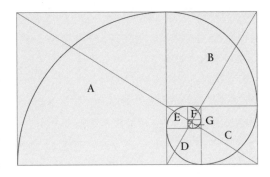

Ratio and upon the Fibonacci sequence (itself a close relative to Phi), where each number is the sum of the two preceding ones (0, 1, 1, 2, 3, 5, 8, 13, 21, 34, 55 . . .). This is an excellent spread for checking the creative curve of a project or idea. The cards are laid in a spiral.

First, shuffle and cut your cards, noting the Guide Cards as usual. Next, with the full pack in your hands, count through from the top, laying down the first, second, third, fifth, eighth, thirteenth and twenty-first cards in the positions of the Golden Rectangle, from A to G. The meanings of the card positions are as follows:

A CONCEPTION What is the kernel of your plan?
B GATHERING What must you gather for it?
C GROWTH What enables it to grow?
D REST What wisdom do you gain as it rests?
E REAPPRAISAL What needs modification?
F FINALIZATION What is needed to finish?
G MANIFESTATION What have you made?

SAMPLE READING

Melanie was engaged by a large firm to completely refurbish their business suite. It was a prestigious assignment and she had but a short deadline. Her questions were: '*How am I progressing on this project? Will I meet the deadline?*' Her Guide Cards were *Four of*

Earth/Assembly, *IX Hermit* and *Three of Air/Trials* (reversed), which outlined her difficulties: demanding employers, a need to progress uninterruptedly, and a fear of not
completing on time.

A *Nine of Air/Danger* A great deal of fear was underlying the refurbishment, and this
had clouded Melanie's judgement.

B *X Time* Time was her big concern. She wanted more of it in order to arrive at the
end result in the way that she wished.

C *Two of Earth/Polarity* A bit of give and take would be nice, but in lieu of that
Melanie needed to make good and decisive choices.

D *IV Emperor* (reversed) Waiting upon suppliers and decorators gave her a sense of
impatience and disempowerment. Getting control of her authority was the wisdom
she needed. The rest was down to things coming together.

E *Ace of Water* In the final stages, Melanie had lost sight of the intrinsic beauty of
what she was trying to create. Returning to this sense of harmony would enable her
to get it right.

F *XXI World* By looking again at how her refurbishment would delight guests, she
could keep on target.

G *XX Renewal* (reversed) This card spoke of delays or last-minute reappraisals on
the part of Melanie's employers. It turned out that she completed the job on time but
had to take out a loan because of the procrastination of her employers, who tried to
find fault with her work and paid late.

OVERVIEW Melanie's forced pace was indicative of the business methods of the company she was working for. She had stepped out of her own creative enclave into a com-
petitive, demanding and uncompromising place where her own values were being upset.
If you were Melanie, what metaphors would occur to you from looking at the images
on the cards, considering the issue? Remember that the visual qualities of a spread are
just as important as the text when you interpret. Look at the four macrocosm cards
and read the soul-code: what help is Melanie being offered from these?

THE DESTINY SPREAD

The Destiny spread is a more advanced reading for the explorative reader interested in the soul's code and how it corresponds to the issue in hand. This spread does not give position meanings, and so all cards are read in connection to the issue. This may seem complex, but after a few spreads you will get the idea and uncover very powerful answers to your issues. Leonardo encouraged such a flexible penetrative observation: 'Stop sometimes, observe the stains on walls, the patterns in ash or fire, clouds or mud or whatnot. In these, if you consider them carefully, you will find ... resemblances to landscapes, battles, figures, etc.' The following steps show you how to lay out your cards.

1 Shuffle in your question, cut and consult the Guide Cards.
2 Randomly choose six to ten cards unseen. *Do not turn over your cards, but leave the backs facing you.*
3 With the card-backs facing you, see how many cards will connect to make part of the pattern (each group of connecting cards forms a set). Cards must be flush to each other and not staggered when you connect them. Try to connect any of the symbols (polyhedra) first, and then see if any parts of the roundels connect. Usually at least six cards out of ten will join together, to make one to three sets, with between one and four cards remaining disconnected. Because of the repetitive nature of the design, some cards can be fitted together when rotated upside down: if they can, then rotate them. You may also find that a card can be connected to more than one other card along the same edge, in which case it's up to you to choose which connection to make. Play with the cards until you have one or more connected sets. (NOTE: It is less common to have large sections of the pattern connected.)
4 After contemplating any connected symbols you may have made, turn over the cards so that they are facing upwards (taking care, at this stage, not to rotate any cards in the process, otherwise upright cards will become reversed, and vice versa), but

move them *mirrorwise*, so that your sets remain in their original connections (*see right*).

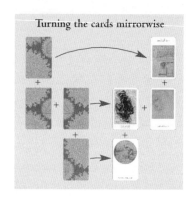

Turning the cards mirrorwise

5 Now study the dynamics of the connected sets. Arrange the sets and disconnected cards in relationship to each other in ways that *you* feel are right. Before looking up meanings, note your first impressions. Try and tell a story about what you see. Notice the different 'acts' in the drama of the unfolding story, especially if you have two or three sets. You may find it helpful to give the sets titles relating to your question or issue (*see sample readings, pages* 140–43).

6 When you begin reading, use only the dimmi questions to start with, to help you understand what answers are given. As you progress, read the upright and reversed meanings of the connected sets first, since these show the part of the soul's code that is strongly operative. Reversed cards represent the ways in which you are struggling to unlock the code by self-will alone, and may indicate areas of blockage. Then read the disconnected cards: these represent the disjected or unintegrated parts of the soul's code to which you currently have no key, but which are important influences that you need to consider. These often show ongoing problems or self-created limitations that keep you disconnected.

7 When you've finished, draw the next unseen card from the pack to act as a 'bridge' between any disconnected cards and one or more parts of the pattern. Consult the Bridge Card's soul-code, for deeper answers that offer corrective guidance. Consider the disconnected card(s) in the new light of the help offered by the Bridge Card(s). (The sample reading on page 142 shows how Bridge Cards work in practice.)

8 Once you've had some practice with looking at the reading in the light of the dimmi questions, then look at the fuller given meanings and cross-relate them, looking at storylines, correspondences, developments and other internal connections.

SUMMARY OF DESTINY SPREAD RULES

- All cards must be flush to each other, not staggered or set horizontally.
- Aim to connect the symbols first, then connect any roundels or parts of roundels. Note which symbols connect.
- Cards may be rotated upside down (creating reversals) in order to connect.
- Connected sets must be turned over mirrorwise so that the connecting patterns remain the same when the cards are face up.
- Arrange the connected sets in ways *you* feel are right.
- Connected sets indicate what is working strongly in the issue.
- Reversed cards indicate what is blocked.
- Disconnected cards indicate self-sabotaging factors or unintegrated soul-trends.
- Start by answering the dimmi questions for each card.
- Notice how the dynamics of your issue run through the cards.
- Cheating by choosing cards to create connections won't give a true reading!

When you are able to connect a symbol (you can usually only connect one, and sometimes none at all), refer to the meanings given in the following table, to give you the perspective from which to interpret your reading. To begin with, you may find you mistake Dodecahedrons with Icosahedrons when you are trying to join your cards, but you will quickly see the difference if you look out for the pentagons of the Dodecahedron and the triangles of the Icosahedron (*see page 17 for more on the polyhedra*).

Before you read on through the interpretations given for the following examples, lay out the cards for each sample reading and try interpreting the cards yourself before reading the interpretation. This is a great way to learn how to use this spread.

	Polyhedron	Number of faces	Element	Meaning	Look at your issue:
	Hexahedron	6 squares	Earth	Stability	Pragmatically
	Tetrahedron	4 triangles	Fire	Flexibility	Passionately
	Octahedron	8 triangles	Air	Penetration	Intelligently
	Icosahedron	20 triangles	Water	Reflection	Mercifully
	Dodecahedron	12 pentagons	Spirit	Wholeness	Wholistically

SAMPLE READING I

Rob is at university reading physics. Towards the end of his final year, a great opportunity to work in an international company arises. This job invitation comes via an acquaintance of the family. Rob wants to finish his finals, but the offer comes with handles: he must start work at least two months before his finals. His question was: *'What are the consequences of taking the job?'*

Guide Cards: *Lady of Fire • Page of Air • XV Pain & Pleasure*

The Guide Cards show a situation with lots of ambivalent emotion, a demanding employer and a need to be very vigilant indeed. Rob's ten cards yield one connected symbol, the Hexahedron, advising him to read the spread pragmatically, and by rotating some of the cards he is able to connect two sets, with no disconnected cards. He carefully turns the sets mirrorwise. The cards of Danger and Death in the second line alarm him, but he notes down the meanings of these cards and ponders the pattern he has made and what it is telling him about the situation. He decides to answer the questions posed by each of the cards under the dimmi headings, and apply his own answers to the situation.

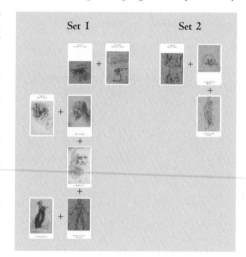

Set I. He entitles this set 'Dynamics of the Job Offer'.

Nine of Earth/Roots (reversed) Where is your rightful place? What attitude must you take? Rob feels that the post is his rightful place, but he knows that this mature place is not yet rightfully his, and the reversal bids him beware of the honeyed trap of security.

Nine of Water/Airborne (reversed) What's your heart's desire? Rob wants this job more than anything.

Nine of Air/Danger (reversed) What do you fear? Do you flee or fight? He fears both losing the opportunity and taking it.

XIII Death What obstructs you? What needs to pass? Getting to finals has been a long struggle to culminate his studies. But he isn't finished yet.

I Magician How does your unique gift change the world? How do you practise and maintain your skills? Rob feels his skills will make a difference, and he is raring to show the world how.

XI Experience How does experience inform integrity? Where do you need to be impartial? The pointing girl shows him an unknown future, but he doesn't want to go there without some better grounding on his own terms.

Seven of Fire/Success What's in your favour? Where must you back down? The cards are in his favour, but he is his own man.

Set 2. He entitles this set 'Consequences of Acceptance'.

Two of Air/Respect (reversed) Where is the balance of respect? With a sinking feeling he answers this truthfully: the job has been offered to him through nepotism not through proven skill. He asks who will respect him if he is not properly qualified? What will become of him if that powerful friend leaves the firm?

Six of Water/Memory How does this call from the past pave the way to the future? He briefly projects what it will be like to be in power and is flooded by a sense of rightness. A slight family connection may not be part of his way forward.

Three of Air/Trials What are you mourning? What is painful? His passage into the everyday world is a struggle. Each of these questions has subtly helped him assess where he stands. Even as a new vista arises within, he has already said goodbye to the job. He would rather spend a couple of years working abroad in the Third World than be some company crony of his father's friend.

INTERPRETATION NOTES Note how in Set I Rob has three reversed Nines – all cards of deferred accomplishment. *XI Experience* and *Seven of Fire/Success* are joined together on the bottom line, giving a firm foundation, but the combination of *Nine* of *Air/Danger* and *XIII Death* over *I Magician* suggests that, without his roots in experience, Rob is merely a sorcerer who courts the death and danger that shriek from the middle line.

SAMPLE READING 2

Andrea's long marriage to Paolo is at an impasse. Their last child is about to leave home and Paolo wants to sell up and move back to his home town in Italy. Andrea doesn't want to go, but her husband has set everything in progress regardless. She asked: *'Help me to see the situation clearly.'*

Guide Cards: *Seven of Earth/Stamina* • *Eight of Earth/Labour* • *Lord of Earth (reversed)*
Andrea's Guide Cards speak of a great deal of effort and labour concerning a man who is mean and manipulative. From the ten cards she chose, she creates three connected sets and has one disconnected card. She has no connected symbols. She titled the three sets after she had concluded the reading.

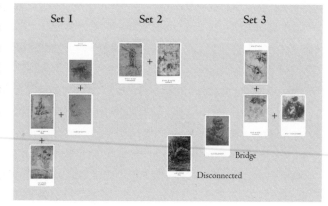

Set I. Setback.
Nine of Earth/Roots (reversed) warns Andrea to be careful of falling into a need for security above everything else, asking 'Where is your rightful place?' It is over *Page of Earth*, which shows Andrea as too trusting. *Five of Earth/Need* shows stark need over *Six of Air/Flowering*, which is often a card of travel or moving on. It asks her about her attitudes and beliefs, which — where marriage has been concerned — are very conventional and dutiful.

Set 2. Reappraisal.

The set of *Eight of Air / Confinement* and *Four of Earth / Assembly* is sandwiched between the unfortunate events outlined in the first set and the solutions of the third set. *Eight of Air* underlines how she is bound by beliefs about her marriage, while *Four of Earth* asks her 'Who is controlling what?', and challenges her to stand her ground. Paolo is using their joint assets to make this move, with money she brought to the marriage.

Set 3. Power struggle.

This set shows a head-to-head between *Page of Fire* (reversed) and *Five of Fire / Struggle*, which reveals a strong struggle within Andrea herself. Her lack of action is at odds with her need to stand up for herself. The only way out is to look at her dreams and test intuitively for the right way. *XVIII Conception* invites her to consult her dreams and intuitions.

Disconnected Card The disconnected *Ace of Fire* shows an alarming detachment from her passion and enthusiasm. The soul-code paragraph gives her advice, but how will she use it?

Bridge Card Andrea drew *V Hierophant* as a Bridge Card to connect her disconnected *Ace of Fire* to Set 3, which is where she felt she most needed it. From this, she felt she could find the authority to follow her most deeply held beliefs and the power not to follow her husband's lead.

INTERPRETATION NOTES Two to three sets of connections are common. Note how many Earth cards come up in this leaving-home issue, including the Guide Cards. What does this signify? See how the disconnected card sits like a slow fuse under the whole reading – what is Andrea not using that would most help her?

BIBLIOGRAPHY AND FURTHER READING

Leonardo Books

Cassirer, Ernst, Paul O. Kristeller & J. H. Randall Jr. *The Renaissance Philosophy of Man*, Chicago, University of Chicago Press, 1948

Da Vinci, Leonardo. *Codex Atanticus*, Milan, Giovanni Piumati, 1894–1904

Da Vinci, Leonardo. *The Codex Leicester: Notebook of a Genius*, ed. & trans. Michael Desmond & Carlo Pedretti, Sydney, Australia, Powerhouse Publishing, 2000

Da Vinci, Leonardo, *Codex Trivulzi*, Milan, Luca Beltrami, 1891

Da Vinci, Leonardo. *The Notebooks*, ed. & trans. Irma K. Richter, Oxford, Oxford University Press, 1998

Da Vinci, Leonardo. *Trattato della Pittura*, Vienna, H. Ludwig, 1882

Kemp, Martin. *Leonardo*, Oxford, Oxford University Press, 2004

Livio, Mario. *The Golden Ratio*, London, Headline Book Publishing, 2002

della Mirandola, Pico. *On the Dignity of Man*, trans. C. G. Wallis, Indianapolis, Bobbs Merril Educational Publishing, 1965

Nicholl, Charles. *Leonardo da Vinci: Flights of the Mind*, London, Allen Lane, 2004

Ovason, David. *The Two Children*, London, Century, 2001

Richter, J. P. *The Literary Works of Leonardo da Vinci*, Oxford, Oxford University Press, 1939

Strathern, Paul. *The Medici: Godfathers of the Renaissance*, London, Pimlico, 2005

White, Michael. *Leonardo, The First Scientist*, London, Little, Brown and Co., 2000

Tarot Books

Greer, Mary. *The Complete Book of Tarot Reversals*, Minnesota, Llewellyn Books, 2002

Greer, Mary. *Tarot for Your Self*, Franklin Lakes, New Jersey, New Page Books, 2002

Kaplan, Stuart R. *Tarot Classic*, New York, Gosset & Dunlap, 1972

Matthews, Caitlín. *The Celtic Wisdom Tarot*, Rochester, VT, Inner Traditions, 1999

Matthews, Caitlín & John. *The Arthurian Tarot*, London, Harper Collins, 1990

Pollack, Rachel. *The Forest of Souls*, Minnesota, Llewellyn Books, 2003

Pollack, Rachel. *Seventy-Eight Degrees of Wisdom*, London, Thorsons, 1997

ACKNOWLEDGEMENTS

Author's Acknowledgements
First of all, huzzas for John for dreaming up the idea and sorry you couldn't come along too. Respect and blessings to Rachel Pollack for continuing tarot symposia and to R. J. Stewart for qabalistic clarity. Great thanks to all at Eddison Sadd for their boundless enthusiasm, expertise and support in helping to create this tarot. Lastly, a deep gratitude to Leonardo for revealing the wisdom of his experience. All quotations from his notebooks and letters are my own translations.

Illustration Sources
Ashmolean Museum, Oxford/Bridgeman Art Library: 102.
Biblioteca Ambrosiana, Milan: 77 (*detail*), 90, 91 (*detail*), 104, 113 (*detail*).
Biblioteca Nacional, Madrid: 100, 101, 112.
Biblioteca Reale, Turin/Alinari: 40, 82 (*detail*), 123.
Biblioteca Reale, Turin/Corbis: 26.
Bibliothèque de Institut de France, Paris/Corbis: 74, 76, 105.
Bibliothèque de Institut de France, Paris/RMN: 99 (*detail*), 120.
British Museum, London/HIP/Topham: 32.
Cabinet des Dessins, Louvre/Alinari: 109, 114.
Cabinet des Dessins, Louvre, Paris/Corbis: 62.
Cabinet des Dessins, Louvre, Paris/RMN: 38 (*detail*).
Christ Church, Oxford/Alinari: 54 (*detail*), 115.
Fitzwilliam Museum, Cambridge/Alinari: 122.
Fitzwilliam Museum, Cambridge/Corbis: 52, 70.
Galleria degli Uffizi, Florence/Corbis: 44.
Gallerie dell' Accademia, Venice/Alinari: 50, 73 (*detail*), 75, 86, 106.
Gallerie dell' Accademia, Venice/Bridgeman Art Library: 87.
Gallerie dell' Accademia, Venice/Corbis: 66.

Graphisches Sammlung Albertina, Vienna/AKG Images: 34.
Hamburger Kunsthalle/Alinari: 71.
Hyde Collection, Glen Falls, New York, 1971.71 Cartoon for Mona Lisa © 1503. Attributed to Leonardo da Vinci, Italian, . 1452-1519. Charcoal and graphite, $24\frac{1}{2}$ x 20 in (622 x 508 mm). Photograph by Joseph Levy: front cover, 28.
Musée Bonnat, Bayonne/Corbis: 78.
Museum Boijmans van Beuningen, Rotterdam: 60.
National Gallery, London/Corbis: 36.
The Royal Collection © 2005 HM Queen Elizabeth II.
Photographer EZM: 24, 56 (*detail*), 69 (*detail*), 80, 94, 97, 103 (*detail*), 107, 110, 118 (*detail*), 124.
The Royal Collection, Windsor/Alinari: 30, 46, 72, 79, 89, 93, 95.
The Royal Collection, Windsor/Bridgeman Art Library: 98.
The Royal Collection, Windsor/Corbis: 42, 58, 64 (*detail*), 81, 83 (*detail*), 84, 88, 92, 96, 108, 111, 116, 117 (*detail*), 119, 121.
The Royal Collection, Windsor/Topham: 85.
Santa Maria delle Grazie a Milano/Alinari: 48.

EDDISON•SADD EDITIONS

Editorial Director	Ian Jackson	*Art Director*	Elaine Partington
Managing Editor	Tessa Monina	*Mac Designer*	Malcolm Smythe
Proofreader	Nikky Twyman	*Production*	Sarah Rooney and
Picture Researcher	Diana Morris		Nick Eddison